Zenas E. Feemster

The Traveling Refugee

Or, the cause and cure of the rebellion in the United States; embracing a sketch of

the state of society in the South, before, and at the commencement of the

rebellion. Illustrated by facts and incidents

Zenas E. Feemster

The Traveling Refugee

Or, the cause and cure of the rebellion in the United States; embracing a sketch of the state of society in the South, before, and at the commencement of the rebellion. Illustrated by facts and incidents

ISBN/EAN: 9783337315269

Printed in Europe, USA, Canada, Australia, Japan

Cover: Foto ©Andreas Hilbeck / pixelio.de

More available books at **www.hansebooks.com**

THE TRAVELING REFUGEE;

OR THE

CAUSE AND CURE OF THE REBELLION

IN THE

UNITED STATES;

EMBRACING A SKETCH

OF THE

STATE OF SOCIETY IN THE SOUTH,

BEFORE, AND AT THE COMMENCEMENT

OF THE REBELLION.

Illustrated by Facts and Incidents.

BY REV. ZENAS E. FEEMSTER, REFUGEE,

FROM MISSISSIPPI, IN 1862.

SPRINGFIELD, ILLS.
STEAM PRESS OF BAKER & PHILLIPS.
1865.

Entered according to Act of Congress in the year 1865, by ZENAS E. FEEMSTER, in the Clerk's Office of the District Court of the United States for the Southern District of Illinois.

PREFACE.

Questions, such as the following, will no doubt often be asked :

Of what does your book treat? What gave rise to it, and what is the object of it? The title page furnishes a clue to the proper answer ; to which I briefly add, that if I know my own heart the prime object has been to do my duty to God, myself and my fellow beings, and to promote the general welfare of my country, politically, morally and religiously : to advance the temporal, spiritual and eternal interests of the human family.

The circumstances which have surrounded me where my lot has been cast, have circumscribed my opportunities for usefulness, in this line, to very narrow limits, which has been a source of mortification of feeling and anxiety of mind. These things, in connection with other considerations, led me to this work, with the hope that through this medium I might have access for good to the minds of many, whom otherwise I never could reach, and thus benefit some where my face can never be seen, nor my voice be heard ; and that, too, when the footsteps of time, in its long march, shall have so erased from earth the visible signs of its present inhabitants that the resting places of most of their mortal remains will be unknown to the living.

As this work contains over twice as much as at first was anticipated, I find, on reviewing my labor, that some of the subjects might be condensed and the work abreviated and improved by a reconstruction of some of its parts, which my circumstances will not permit me to do.

I am aware that the work abounds with imperfections, and that there may be many things in it to which men of science and taste can take exception; yet, I flatter myself that if subjected to a scientific ordeal, the unfavorable circumstances under which it was written, while changing from place to place, often surrounded with scenes of noise and confusion, and other contingencies calculated to perplex and distract the mind, in connection with the following facts, will afford a sufficient apology to screen those imperfections from the severe censure of the scientific; at least the liberal and generous among them who have been favored with superior advantages.

I was born in South Corolina, A. D. 1813. Was taken by my parents to Tennessee in 1819, and to the state of Mississippi i in 1820. Went to school about three months in the summer and fall of 1824, and about the same length of time in the winter of 1830, and acquired the remainder of my education at home. In July, 1862 went to Illinois; in the following spring went to, and spent several weeks with the Union soldiers, at Corinth and Glendale, Mississippi, returned in the summer to Illinois, and spent from that time to this date in Illinois and Indiana.

March 31, 1865.

TABLE OF CONTENTS.

	PAGE.
CHAPTER I.—State of Society in the South before the Rebellion	9
CHAPTER II.—Slavery and Condition of Slaves in the South—The General Opinion of People Concerning the Institution—Ways of Justifying it—Notions Concerning the Capacities and Origin of the Negro	43
CHAPTER III.—Personal Concerns and Incidents	53
CHAPTER IV.—Incidents Illustrating the Notions of Southern People at the Beginning of the Confederacy	69
CHAPTER V.—Time, Manner and Circumstance of Escape from the South—Incidents by the Way—At the Union Lines—Meeting with Refugee Friends	92
CHAPTER VI.—Occurrences on the Way from Tuscumbia, Ala., to Mount Zion, Ill	113
CHAPTER VII.—First fall and Winter's Experience in the North—Return to Corinth—Incidents of the Way	124
CHAPTER VIII.—Occurrences at Corinth and Glendale—Distressing News from Home—Return to Macon Co., Ill	137
CHAPTER IX.—Travels and Occurrences in the North—From Indiana to Southern Illinois—Letters from a Nephew forced into Service in the Union Army, at Camp Davis, Miss	146
CHAPTER X.—Incidents of Travels while Canvassing Kansas, Grandview, Embarrass and Buck Townships in Edgar Co., Ill	169
CHAPTER XI.—Cause, Cure and Prevention of Division, War and National Calamity	176
The Egyptian Song	181
Refugees Parody	186
Parting Scene	187
Wandering Refugee	190
Prospective Vision	193

*—1

Those who abide in my word,
   Are my disciples indeed,
And those who believe in the Lord,
   Thereby are Abraham's seed.

Those who obey his holy word,
   (Let him that readeth understand,)
Shall see the glory of the Lord,
   And eat the good of all the land.

Now he that hath ears let him hear,
   But if they refuse and rebel,
Remember the truth that I say,
   The sword shall their wickedness quell,
Devour and take them away,
   Upon them shall be their own fear!

THE TRAVELING REFUGEE.

CHAPTER I.

STATE OF SOCIETY IN THE SOUTH BEFORE THE REBELLION.

For the space of twenty years past, or more, it appears that morality has generally been on the decline in the south, though in many localities there have been happy exceptions, where progress and improvement have developed themselves; yet these exceptions were so few and far between, as to afford but little restraint upon society. Though the youth had many advantages for scientific and literary attainments above their parents, yet, with a supposed higher and more refined state of society, scripture morality was falling into disrepute. The young generally manifested little regard and veneration for the aged; and though the curse of God is pronounced against those who set lightly by father or mother, yet those who did so were evidently becoming very numerous, and those who cursed them were not a few, and the number that vainly used the name of the Lord, among some professed Christians, was not small, while many were guilty of the sin of intoxication. Parental authority over their children was exercised to a very limited extent, and children, at a very early period, thought themselves beyond the time of chastisement, and parental restraint, and soon concluded that they must have a purse of their own, have a claim to property, and exercise authority, while popular custom authorized and encouraged the practice. They professed themselves superior to, and often mistreated those whom they frequently compelled to participate in the most degrading vices. Thereby, the downtrodden victims of their wickedness were subjected to a mortifying sense of their unavoidable degradation. Yet many such occupied high places, figured largely and made a display in society, though destitute of virtue, pride of character and all the principles of elevated humanity.

Thus, a part of the inhabitants of the south, whose guilt or misfortune it was to have a black skin, or to have descended from those who had, were placed under circumstances calculated to corrupt, and crush out every principle and mark of moral honesty or excellence. A gross departure from the pure principles of refinement, (mildness, kindness and gentleness of manners,) extensively prevailed among the young of all classes, both bond and free. The aged of both classes would generally meet each other with marks of respect and civility, kindly giving place to the just, equal rights of others, manifesting a disposition to impart any useful information they could that might be desired; while the young would expect others to give place to them, though much older than themselves; and would frequently give rough and impolite answers to civil questions, and rough salutations to those whom they met. They were impatient undey restraint, easily provoked, disposed to impose much on others, restless under rebuke and despisers of reproof. They were quick to find fault with others, but would bear but little themselves. The Sabbath was a day little regarded by a majority of the people, as the holy of the Lord, honorable, and by which they would honor him, not doing their own ways, nor finding their own pleasure, nor speaking their own words ; while a few spent the day in attending church and in religious employments at home, but more spent their Sabbaths in visiting, sleeping, worldly conversation, gaming, hunting, frolicing or attending market.

No sacred day of just employ,
For heavenly treasure ;
A chosen time for carnal joy,
And sensual pleasure.

The Sabbath in the south was often a hard day on the sick, the waiter and the cook. It was quite common with some to congregate on the Sabbath for singing ; and if a teacher taught on the Sabbath day gratis, he was considered quite generous for giving a day that did not belong to him, though he thereby robbed God. Sometimes singing associations, though good in their place, became so absorbing as to supercede, to some extent, the Gospel ministry. Crowds would attend them, even from a distance, to the neglect of the Gospel. Anything that is substituted for a divine institution must meet with the Divine disapprobation.

The use of profane language was shockingly and shamefully prevalent in the south.

Fornication and adultery were developed, not only in the varied shades of servants, but in numerous other things that were astonishing and mortifying to the pure minded.

The excess of vanity and fashion, that added nothing to decency, convenience or comfort, the saving of labor, time or expense, swept all before it—like the frogs of Egypt, defiling every place with their pollution. Yet there were those who lamented it, and raised their voice against it, feeling the necessity of temperance in all things; and were willing, to some extent, to be counted singular for the sake of divine precepts, though their names should be cast out as evil.

The forms of religion were in the various denominations; and doubtless there were many truly pious and useful members in every relation, who would have been an honor to good society in any age or country. And some churches and congregations appeared to be generally composed of such; yet these were great exceptions to the general state of things, making the Scriptures the rule to judge by; for while in many places the people were nearly all professors of religion and members of some church, the state of things that existed among them generally, was but too well described by the prophets.

In speaking of the corrupt and backslidden state of religion, Isaiah says, chap. I, 21, 22, 23, "How is the faithful city become a harlot. It was full of judgment, righteousness lodged in it; but now murderers. Thy silver is become dross, thy wine mixed with water; thy princes are rebellious, and companions of thieves; every one loveth gifts and followeth after rewards; they judge not the fatherless, neither doth the cause of the widow come unto them." Sam. IV, 1, says: "How is the gold become dim; how is the most fine gold changed. The precious sons of Zion, comparable to fine gold, how are they esteemed as earthen pitchers. He that departeth from iniquity maketh himself a prey." And Paul says in II Timothy, III chap.: "For men shall be lovers of their own selves, covetous, boasters, proud, blasphemers, disobedient to parents, unthankful, unholy, without natural affection, truce breakers, false accusers, incontinent, fierce despisers of those that are good, traitors, heady, high minded, lovers of pleasure more than lovers of God, having a form of godliness, but denying the power thereof." In Jer. IX, 2, it is said: "Oh! that I had in the wilderness a lodging place of wayfaring men; that I might leave my people and go from them, for they be all adulterers and assembly of treacherous men. They bend their tongue like their bow, for lies; but they are not valiant for the truth upon the earth, for they proceed from evil to evil, and they know not me, saith the Lord. Take heed every man of his neighbor, and trust ye not in any brother; for every brother will utterly supplant, and every neighbor will walk with slanderers; and they will deceive every one his neighbor, and will not speak the truth; they have taught their tongue to speak lies, and weary themselves to commit iniquity; one speaketh peaceably with his neighbor, but with his heart he layeth his wait."

Many made show of religion when at church, especially on revival occasions, as they were called, but on other occasions were hard to distinguish from non-professors. Frequently the difference could be discerned only on sacramental occasions. They were as anxious about the things of the world, their conversation as much about them, and in their lives as much. Conformed to its maxims, fashions and practice as others. They could well afford to be religious, while they were not thereby prevented from carrying the world in their arms, enjoying its treasures, honors and pleasures, and were not required to walk after the example, and according to the precepts of Christ and his apostles; or to bear the cross and deny themselves of all ungodliness and worldly lusts, as taught by him who came not to do his own pleasure, but the will of Him who sent him, and to take upon him the form of a servant and became poor, that we through his poverty might be made rich. Thereby, they were liable to become unpopular, and lose the friendship of the world, to be reproached and have their names cast out as evil. They were soon offended, and the church, and the cause of Christ, might take care of themselves. Many of those who were liable to church censure, would apply for a recommendation or dismissal, that they might join other churches, many of which were willing to receive them, in order to swell their number. Many had great zeal in promoting the interests of the sect to which they belonged, in defending their peculiar doctrines and practices, making converts to their party. Their spirits were stirred within them at anything said or done against them; while they could see the weightier matters of the law disregarded, and Gospel precepts trampled upon; and even participate in the same without having their religious feelings mortified.

It had long been customary, at certain seasons of the year, to hold camp, or protracted meetings, to which they looked forward for revivals, and the idea was growing more general that these were the only occasions on which much good was to be accomplished; and little was expected from a single sermon, or one day's meeting; and hence, they were, to a great extent, unprepared for obtaining a blessing by them. But camp meetings, once so abundantly marked with the manifestations of the presence and the blessing of God, when they were devoted wholly to His service, had become so perverted that they were almost entirely dispensed with, from the fact, that instead of being a time devoted exclusively to His worship and cause, they were times of display, feasting and the entertainment of friends, among the fashionable. These meetings became the resort of the vile, seeking pleasure and amusements in the indulgence of their appetites and passions, and added greatly to the burdens of those by whom supplies and accommodations were provided. Then came protracted meetings, with the growing persuasion that they were mainly to be depended upon for revivals, conversions, &c. To these the people of the surrounding neighborhood went, with provisions for themselves. This they called a basket meeting or dinner, of which they all partook during the intervals of worship. Dinner was sometimes placed upon a common table, and a general invitation given to all present to come and partake. Here some made a great display of generosity in distributing that among their friends which they themselves had not provided; and was frequently an occasion for unpleasant feelings. At other times they would go to their wagons, carriages, and chosen places, and invite and select their guests. Here, too, often were seen selfishness, ostentation and pride; those foul worms whose touch defiles and blasts every benevolent, moral and religious enterprise; mars every good work, and poisens every cup of heavenly bliss. It was evident that many of the attendants were like the Jews, of whom the Savior said, they follow him, not because they saw his miracles, but for the loaves and fishes. People were getting too nice and fine to carry supplies with them to sustain nature till they returned home, as they formerly did, when they thought more of their souls, and less of their appetites and dress. Those who furnished supplies for those at a distance, often entertained many who were as convient as themselves; and if this were not done feelings were injured, and remarks made, not intended to add to honor or respectability. It was also customary in some places, when meetings were held for preaching at private houses, that so many remained for dinner that it became a very heavy tax on the good man of the house; so that judicious, humane ministers were constrained sometimes to discontinue their appointments, rather than to give occasion for the poor but warm hearted friends to the cause of Christ to be so wantonly imposed upon, by the unprincipled, thoughtless and imprudent.

While things were going on in this way, and the minds of men much absorbed in the general pursuit of wealth, fashionable display, pleasure and sensual indulgence, the sentiment prevailed among many of the ministers, as well as with the common people, that nothing could effect any good with the people then, but something of the most stirring, impressive and startling nature; hence sermons and forms of religious services were gotten up, with an eye to moving upon and exciting the passions; and many institutions were adopted, and secret organizations, promising greatly to improve and ameliorate the condition of man, and advance the cause of religion. It was also quite evident that while these things were progressing, a departure from the primitive purity and simplicity of the Gospel, and strict conformity to Bible precept were making equal advances. True religion, with a consistent daily walk in the life and power of the same, was superceded by a profession without fruits meet for repentance, and a form of godliness without the power; as the latter rose and progressed, the former fell and lost reputation and respectability; just as the customs, doctrines and traditions of men were put in the place of the institutions and doctrines of Christ; just in proportion as they trusted to man and his devices, instead of God and his appointed means, and also, departed from the fountain of living waters and hewed out cisterns of their own.

Many very exciting discourses and excuses were resorted to to get up revivals or religious excitement, while the plain instructions which ignorant people always need, were very much neglected; and more was done to move feelings and excite passions, than to instruct and enlighten the mind and correct the judgment with regard to the fundamental doctrines of the Gospel. Hence, the notion too generally prevailed that religion consists in strong feeling and lively fancies, instead of a radical change of heart, and an abiding and established principle of holiness and rectitude, produced and kept up by the word and spirit of God and the co-operation of man, by acquiescence in the Divine will.

Many revivals of this kind were gotten up from year to year, and many were reported to have been converted at those meetings, insomuch that in some places, for a while after those occasions, nearly all were professors of religion. But it often so happened that in less than a year, and sometimes, in a few weeks, a large portion of them were ready for the same process again, and occupying a looser and wilder position in society than before; yet frequently, in the course of a few years, making new professions of religion, and joining sometimes the same, and sometimes another church, and, in some instances, taking a stand on the side of infidelity, professing to have experienced all that anyone else had, and to know that it was all a delusion, without any reality in it.

Sometimes those great and far-famed revivalists brought such reproach upon the cause as much aided the pretensions of apostates to infidelity, who, as the apostle said, if they had been of us, would, no doubt, have remained with us.

When those revivals were in progress, persons who kept within the bounds of moderation were looked upon by many as cold hearted, formal and unfeeling, and as weak and not very bright christians; while those who made much noise and show, and were very forward, in the popular way, were the ones to be trusted to for effecting much in the way of conversions. The man who had a strong voice, and could speak and sing loudly, and make a great show of feeling, tell a moving story and teach repentance (undefined,) fervent, persevering prayer, &c., but said little to move the conscience, convict of sin, and lead to true penitence and submission to Christ—was the great preacher with the majority; while those who contrasted the heart and actions of man with the word of God, and showed what man in his unrenewed state is, by nature and by practice; and what he must be by grace, to be happy in the presence and government of God; that the rebel against the Divine government must lay down his weapons of rebellion, surrender himself to the Lord, accept of salvation at his hand, as a free unmerited gift, acquiescing in the Divine plan, trusting in Christ as his only Savior, confiding in his atonement made on the cross as the only meritorious grounds of hope, of pardon and salvation, and that upon this condition, which is FAITH, or BELIEVING IN CHRIST, he enters into a covenant relation with God, which secures renovation or sanctification to the believer, whereby he becomes a new creature in Christ Jesus; renewed in the temper and spirit of his mind to the moral image of God, with the law written in his heart, which gives a delight in, and a desire to practice that which is holy, just and good; a qualification, without which no man can enjoy fellowship with God, or be happy in time or eternity. And until our pride is so humbled, our stubborn, self-willed, rebellious disposition, so subdued and broken down, that we renounce the world, give up our sinful pleasures and pursuits, and honestly and heartily commit and submit ourselves to Christ, no longer to be our own, but the servants of him who has bought us with his own blood, and thus, so far, become partakers with the divine nature or the spirit of Christ; that we can deny ourselves, take up our cross and follow him through evil or good report, it matters not what our feelings, religious professions and pretensions may be, our hope is built upon a sandy foundation, and is a delusion that will leave us a wretched wreck of ruins and hopeless disappointment. The man who did as the prophets were directed to do, (Isa. LVIII. " Cry aloud and spare not; lift up thy voice like a trumpet and show my people their transgressions." Ezra XXXIII, 6, 7,) and warned the people from the Lord, and honestly and faithfully told them the consequences of their evil ways, was often suspected of being personal, and generally soon became unpopular, and had few to hear him; especially if he spoke against the sins that were highly esteemed by the devotees of fashion and high style of life, though ever so abominable in the sight of God. But the man man who prophesied smooth things and deceits, healed the hurt of the daughter of Zion slightly, crying peace, peace, when there was no peace; often pronouncing those righteous whose actions soon proved them to be "the wicked, to whom there is no peace, saith my God, but they are like the troubled sea when it cannot rest, whose waves cast up mire and dirt"—HE was the people's preacher—HE was the popular one, who could lament the calamity of the fall, the cruel ravages of death, bereaving the tender mother of her more tender and innocent offspring, severing all the tenderest ties of dearest friends and relations, producing the many affecting death bed scenes and heart rending bereavements, ushering the pale victim into the silent, gloomy tomb, a putrifaction and decomposition, but said little to reprove or rebuke sin or arouse the conscience of the guilty, or if he did, showed by his own actions a strong sympathy and lively relish for the same. Such a one was a chosen vessel for delivering funeral sermons; who generally made a flattering discourse concerning the dead, and preached them safe to a better home.

In their meetings, they often had little regard to the apostolic rule—that all things should be done decently and in order, and to edification—that prophets should prophesy by two or three, and that by turn, (one at a time.)

Often at the close of a sermon, or a sermon and an exortation, both of which, according to popular opinion should be very short, (and which frequently had as much, and sometimes more of the altar and anxious bench in them than of Christ and him crucified), an invitation would be given to the anxious, or seekers, to come forward to the altar or anxious bench, while a hymn was being sung, that the christians might pray for them; encouraging them to come forward, saying that many had obtained religion in that way, or by that means, and sometimes would spend as much time exhorting and persuading people to come forward to the altar of prayer, as they did preaching, and have heard the statement made: " There are persons here who are powerful in prayer; they are fair Benjamites in prayer; they can almost pray heaven and earth together;" and they were encouraged to avail themselves of so favorable an opportunity. If none would come forward, then christians were sometimes invited to come forward, if they wished an interest in the prayers of the church; and propositions were

*—2

offered for making vows, covenant engagements, &c.—all with an eye to the great object of a revival and the conversion of sinners.

I once witnessed the following arrangement, when previous efforts had failed to effect the desired object; Seats were set apart, one for those who wished to go to heaven; another for those who were determined to go to hell; and each class invited to come forward and accupy his seat. Some coming in afterward and not knowing the arrangement, found it convenient to occupy what was called the devil's seat till their misfortune was revealed to them. When they could succeed in getting people forward, sometimes a prayer would be offered for them in hearing of all, so that all who had the heart to do so could unite and acquiesce in the prayer made by the leader; and all could be edified and say amen, at the close of the prayer; after which some persons would go and converse with and instruct the seekers individually.

But this order was often superceded by a very different practice: When mourners were called forward, then the christians were requested to come and kneel around them, as near as they could, then one would be called upon to lead in prayer, and perhaps a half or a whole dozen, or more, would strike in at the top of their voices, so that, unless the leader had a strong voice, he would be so excelled by others as to be heard by few. Some would be clapping their hands and shouting, some crying one thing and some another, and there was reason to fear that many of them had very few rational, well connected thoughts upon any very profitable subject.

Had the leaders themselves any very important business to transact, upon the correctness of which much of their worldly interests depended, they would have sought circumstances of more quietude and composure, as the most favorable to avoid the damage and loss liable to be sustained by error or mistake. Yet these were the scenes and circumstances labored and sought for, and recommended by them as the most favorable for transacting that business upon which the eternal destiny of man is suspended.

Frequently christians were all strongly urged to go to their relations, friends and neighbors, and talk with them and persuade them to go to be prayed for. In some instances persons were forcibly lead forward, and sometimes the sentence of backslider, cold hearted, graceless professor was passed upon such as would take no part in such a course, because they thought it unscriptural, uncalled for and unjustifiable.

Sometimes christians generally were requested to talk to and instruct those who came forward for prayer. Young converts were encouraged to occupy this office, and also to lead in prayer, though sometimes among the most ignorant and illiterate, and destitute to a shameful degree of scripture knowledge; and those who were the most forward on these occasions were frequently far from being the most forward on other occasions, to set an example consistent with, and honoring to their profession.

The following are some of the instructions given on these occasions: Pray on mourners—pray fervently—never give over. Believe that the Lord will save you and he will do it. Surrender yourself to Christ—commit your all to him. Commit all into his hands, and trust to him alone. Divers other instructions were given, and frequently, like Job's messengers, before one had finished his story another would begin; and he that was inquiring for the way, wishing to know what to do to be saved, had to make the best of the mixture he could, and according to his faith, so went the case with him; whether he trusted to his own, or other people's prayers, his feelings, repentance, or in Christ, according to the safety of the foundation was his hope.

While some, to some extent, brought forth fruit meet for repentance, to others, it happened according to the true proverb of the dog and the sow, they were soon found participating in scenes of dissipation and excess, staggering or prostrate in the street or by the highway side, or in low and groveling deeds of trifling mischief: dishonestly and depradations upon neighbors' farms, orchards, vineyards, utensils for labor, unfinished work, &c.; and it sometimes so happened, that of such as these were those who a short time before had more religion than they well knew what to do with; and by their activity and zeal, in the fashionable way, had procured for themselves great applause and renown, and left far behind in the dark shades of disrepute those whose moral and christian course in life had been like the stream that flows uniformly and gently forth from an unfailing fountain, silently imparting a refreshing and invigorating influence along its margin, wherever it winds its beneficent course among the trees, shrubs and plants of earth.

If a man was wealthy and contributed liberally to the call of the church, he was not in much danger of being turned out of the church for disorderly conduct, though quite irregular in his conduct. But if poor, he might chance to fare like Jonah in the vessel.

While some did not approve of the manner of conducting religious worship, and thought them anti-scriptural, without precept or precedent in the Bible, and productive of consequences pernicious and ruinous to pure religion and the best interests of the church, others thought, as did the town clerk of Ephesus with regard to the worship of Diana: that these things could not be spoken against; and like the Jews in the days of our Savior, who preferred the commandments and doctrines of men, to the commandments of God, and made void the law of God that they might keep their own traditions; so many appeared to prefer those arrangements and traditions of men, to the appointments of God, and to depend more upon them than upon the preaching of the Gospel, which was ordained to be the wisdom and power of God unto salvation. Many who were very tenacious of those customs and could not bear to hear them spoken against, made no matter of conscience of desecrating the Sabbath or taking the advantage of a neighbor in a trade, or neglecting to train their children, by precept and practice, to live according to scripture rules; and could hear the name of God blasphemed, see his commandments violated and trodden under foot, without manifesting much, if any, sense of mortication or disapprobation of the outrage. There were many perhaps in all denominations who had great zeal for the peculiar doctrines, customs and external modes of their favorite sect, while they passed lightly over many of the weightier matters of the law and Gospel; and gave little evidence of much experience in the life and power of true godliness. Yet it added much in their estimation to a man's capacity, intelligence, integrity and veracity to belong to their party. Some were depending upon their morality and upright dealing with their neighbor; some were strict keepers of the Sabbath, though of rare occurrence, but not very exemplary on other occasions—of whom it was contemptuously said: "They kept the Sabbath day holy and cursed all the week; that they were saints on the Sabbath and devils all the week." Had they been devils all the time, it would appear they could have no objections to them, but being right in one good thing, (which they ought to have done, and not to have left the others undone), in this they were a reproof to those who were opposed to being restrained on the Sabbath; and, in reality, they disliked them on that account, and not so much because they did wrong all the week, as because they did right on the Sabbath, which was a favorite time with them to do wrong, when perhaps if they had learned the true reason of their heartfelt opposition to those hypocrites, as they called them, they would have found it really was the same that Cain had for killing his brother.

There was often a show of great zeal among most denominations for benevolent or missionary operations, foreign and domestic. Societies called benevolent were organized to aid in this noble enterprise, for its more successful accomplishment. While there was a great zeal to send missionaries to educate and enlighten those who were perishing for lack of knowledge, also for furnishing every family at home, who would accept of it, with a copy of the scriptures, there was a class whose labors provided the principal means of benevolence in the country, for whose benefit laws were enacted to prevent them from being educated, so as to enable the men to read, and thereby instruct themselves in the doctrines of the Bible. While this class whom they daily saw, and by whose labors they were furnished with the comforts and luxuries of life, were so little cared and provided for in this line, they had great sympathy for those whom they had never seen. While it was a popular and honorable thing to be on the list of liberal donors for charitable and benevolent purposes, how much was done to be seen of men, and for the honor that cometh from man, is only known by Him who knows the secrets of all hearts.

But rich and poor, bond and free, were all called upon to do something in the cause. When the poor contributed it was generally more in proportion to their means than that by the rich, who, of their abundance contributed much.

Some of those who so zealously solicited contributions, were arrayed in costly and high style, and could afford to send their children to high school, and had themselves been enabled by the contributions of the people, to own land and farms and servants; while numbers of the donors were very hard run to get a very limited education, and poorly furnished homes for their families. Yet those who were so zealously affected for the poor, benighted heathen abroad, and benevolent institutions and missions at home, or perhaps for having the honor of raising the largest contributions, in their call, could ask for the poor man's mite, raised by the sale of nuts collected from the forest, and the earnings of the slave that he had procured by his labors on holidays, and at night, after his day's work for his master was done. The poor widow's two mites were often referred to on these occasions, and anecdotes of highly favorable and unexpected and unthought of occurrences taking place with persons, after making liberal contributions: such as unexpected legacy, return of stock given up for lost, lost articles of value being found, &c.

While some were actuated by impure motives, and resorted to unworthy measures to acquire means for good purposes, and those were sometimes put to a bad use; all of which gave occasion to the adversaries to spead reproachfully, and furnished an excuse to many for withholding their aid.

At the same time, there was a class of professed christians who openly and publicly opposed all missionory, bible and tract societies, and Sabbath school operations, and all societies for aiding in benevolent enterprises, and denounced them as anti-scriptural, and represented them as being the beast or the image of the beast, that had seven heads and ten horns; and represented those engaged in those societies as trying to take God's work out of his hands, which he would accomplish in his own good time and way, without their instrumentalities; who were like Uzzah when he put forth his unhallowed hand to stay the ark of the Lord. All were often denounced from the pulpit; and also literary qualifications for the ministry. And many were employed as teachers who could not speak their own mother tongue with any tolerable degree of propriety; and, although they professed to be chosen, called and inspired to preach and to teach the people and expound the scriptures, could not tell the difference between the present and past tense of the verb read; but could gesticulate as though they would throw their limbsfrom their bodies, rant, vociferate and bawl as if they would tear their lungs out; and pour forth a tide of incoherent, imperfectly articulated language, and many unmeaning words, such as could be found in none of the dictionaries or standard works in the language of any civilized nation under heaven.

Some delivered their discourses with a vibrating tone or song; others ended their sentences with an insignificant oh, or thrust it in elsewhere to keep up the sound of their whistle, till they had let off their steam and exhausted their physical strength. And oh, they were so feeling and zealous they were highly esteemed as good, great and powerful men by the ignorant and uncultivated, with whom a great noise would pass for logic and gospel; presumption for faith, and a great gust or flow of animal passion for renewing or sanctifying grace. And though these teachers had never read one-fourth part of the Bible regularly through in their lives, nor perhaps one chapter correctly in the New Testament, yet their vulgar speeches and rude criticisms, proceeding from a poorly educated brain, and an undisciplined and unbridled tongue, against refinement, science, the scientific and scientific statements, were heard and received as with open mouth, and eyes widely staring, with wonder and astonishment at, and admiration of their profound reasoning from their amazing depths and hights and inexhaustible treasures of knowledge and divinely inspired skill, in bringing to light the deep and hidden mysteries of God, not generally made known to others as to themselves; and though they knew little of what is in the Bible and of Bible history, and of ancient histories, and, consequently, of the true meaning of much of the New Testament, yet many preferred and depended upon these as teachers and guides, instead of those who like Timothy of old, had known the scriptures from a child, and had studied and practiced them from their youth up, and were well acquainted with the Old and New Testament scriptures, and the history of the times, and the people that lived, and the language spoken by them during those ages in which the scriptures were written, and the customs and practices that obtained and prevailed, which were the foundation of many of the metaphors, parables and comparisons of the scripture, by which many of their important doctrines are illustrated. "If the blind lead the blind, shall they not both fall into the ditch?"

While this state of things prevailed in the rough background of the country, where was often intermixed a sprinkle of the precious of the earth, clothed in native simplicity of style, with the charms of honest, unaffected sweetness of disposition, kindness and gentleness of manner, ornamented with true christian charity—all traceable to the right use of the old family Bible—free from a burden of useless compliments and vain show of fashionable politeness and hollow hearted outward display of friendship and good will, among the wealthy and more highly cultivated, where science, fashion, fancy and extravagance prevailed, the root of all evil was to too great an extent the presiding divinity, in both church and state. Fashion and display were the order of the day, and authorities to high to be called in question or spoke against, without incurring the displeasure of their devotees, in whose estimation a person diminished in proportion to his similarity to the poor wise man, who, for the sake of others, submitted to be more uncomfortably circumstanced in some respects, than the foxes and fowls.

Many of their ministers set an example of indulgence in the lust of the flesh and the eye and the pride of life, but appeared to forget the apostle's plan of preaching: "We preach not ourselves, but Christ Jesus the Lord, and ourselves your servants, for Christ's sake." And "not in the excellency of speech which man's wisdom deviseth."

Some of them delivered their discourses in a style that quite transcended the comprehenison of a majority of their hearers, and so decorated and varnished their discourses with rhetorical figures, flowery flights of oratory, that they appeared to lose sight of everything but to make a display of themselves; as if their object was to obtain for themselves the honor conferred upon Herod, when he made his oration to the Jews.

In their display of superior and towering intellect, and vast scientific attainments in the philosophical and astronomical researches, they could dive down to the unseen regions and focal center of earth's circumferal attraction, and, by power of steam plow fearlessly through the mighty ocean's thundering roar of mountain and wave, ride the submarine telegraph, with electric speed, to the trans-Atlantic shore, to courts, councils and palaces of kings and emperors, and in a vast and towering flight through illimitable space, in admiration of countless systems of worlds that harmoniously play around the central and topless throne of the eternal God, and range through these scenes sublime, but appear to forget and lose sight of the meek and lowly spirit, the humble and condescending example set before the children of men by the great and glorious Maker and Preserver of all, when he came to fulfill his saving mission upon earth;

where he was first found by those who sought not among the rich and scientific at a public inn, or palace of a king, arrayed in princely apparel, but in a manger in a stall, and wrapped in swaddling clothes. Oh, what contempt of the honors of wealth, glory and display of the pride of life, among sinful, infatuated, dying worms of the dust!

While many greatly admired those great men and their flowing displays, of which they comprehended little, those who, as Peter directs, were, as new born babes, desiring the sincere milk of the word, that they might grow thereby, went away hungry and disappointed, as from a thistle or thorn bush, without being nourished and strengthened by refreshing clusters from a fruitful branch of the true-vine.

While such teachers could be heard patiently through a long discourse, by a large crowd of admiring hearers, the man who confined himself to the plain and simple truths of the gospel, and heart searching and soul trying doctrines of the word of God, which is the sword of the spirit, had few to hear him and still fewer to admire his performance; while many complained of the length of his sermons and their lack of interesting matter; and to listen to two on one Sabbath day was intolerable; that many could exclaim from the bottom of their hearts, "What a weariness is it," while there were comparatively few who had a hearty relish for this kind of preaching and manner of spending the Sabbath, and gave evidence of the same by their faithful and regular attendance upon it, there were multitudes who could be highly entertained and deeply interested during the whole day with worldly conversation about their political fancies and parties and pecuniary prospects, while God, judgment and eternity appeared to be not in all their thoughts, but were unwelcome intruders upon those choice seasons of interesting conversation on interesting subjects, seemingly of far more importance to them.

While churches in some places were falling to ruins, and places of religious worship were neglected and forsaken, and appointments for religious duties forgotten, appointments for political harangues and public dinners and shows were recolected and attended by vast multitudes; so that it might be said, "there was no end to their horses and chariots," and one short day would not afford them time enough to get through with their interesting business and enjoyments, and

—3

with suitable alterations, the sublime language of the christian poet could be heartily adopted by a great many:

>My willing heart would gladly stay
> At such a jolly place as this,
>Amuse and sport itself away,
> In endless scenes of carnal bliss
>Away from rigid Bible schools,
> And all the long faced preacher's tales,
>Where the epicurian rules,
> With all the free born race prevails.
>
>Up to this joyful, happy feast,
> We precious gifts have freely sent,
>For here the prophet and the priest,
> Us with their words cannot torment.
>In obscure silence let them weep;
> Reproofs from them we will not bear,
>For since the fathers fell asleep,
> All things remain just as they were.
>
>Away with all their silly hum,
> As if the Lord was near at last,
>And shortly he to earth would come—
> The time is now already past,
>Let all their tales be now forgot,
> So shall sweet joy and mirth begin,
>And let their names and memory rot,
> And be as though they had not been.
>
>Now let us laugh and joyful be,
> For sure we have a jubilee.
>Sure, such a treat we could not miss,
> For this to us is solid bliss.
>
>At this good friend you need not fret,
> For if we can we don't regret.
>The rule with you should always be,
> Your course pursue and so will we.
>
>The choice we make, if ill or well,
> That place we'll take, heaven or hell;
>Nor ever dread time passing by,
> But eat and drink, for soon we die.

As time passed away great changes were made, both in the face of the country and in the disposition and manners of the people, during a period of time in which there was less wealth and fewer facilities for accumulating property, and more plainness of fashion and simplicity of manners prevailed, and much more was produced by labor than there was much demand for in market, and there was little occasion for excitement or emulation upon the subject of wealth, generosity, harmony, friendship, peace and a good degree of temporal policy generally prevailed. The poor and unfortunate were sympathised with, and cared for, and the pleasant state of society might well be compared to a flourishing bed of full grown touch-me-nots, which ornament the scenery and delight the senses with their beauties and rich perfume. But as facilities for wealth increased, and everything that could be made could be turned into money, avarice, covetousness, ambition, vanity, haughtiness, selfishness, emulation, jealousy, strife and division increased in church and state. Neighborhoods and families, government and order, in all their relations and departments in life, were crippled and deranged, and all classes, from the child to persons of mature years, were so inflated with pride and vain notions of themselves, and jealousy for their rights to unrestrained liberty and high honor and reputation, that they were creatures of such magnitude in their own estimation, that it was difficult for me to move about them, without, in their estimation, coming in hostile contact with them, and seriously conflicting with that of which they were so tenacious. A state of society which, instead of the beauty and fragrance of plants, decorated with fresh flowers, is better represented by the old stalk almost stripped of leaves and flowers, but furnished with homely brown pods, (guarded with stiff bristles,) dry and ready to burst at the slightest touch on any part, while inside out throw its seeds in every direction, so that nothing is likely to escape a hit, and when one of those pods is touched, in a moment they all feel it, and with a bounce are whirling and curling inside out, and hurling their contents as with malicious fury and confusion in every direction, so that nothing can escape a hit, and all eyes had better be shut.

Thus people were prepared for acting toward each other, and imaginary and unintended errors in conduct towards a person must be honorably redressed, explained and atoned for, and the unruly member was let loose.

> A spark now kindle with a breath,
> Hurled brands of fire, shafts and death,
> While others acting out the same,
> Had nature all wrapped in a flame.

And so of chance or desire,
All nature's course was on fire,
More sad and awful still to tell,
The source from which it came is hell.

Most horrid passions of the soul,
All harbored in the human breast,
As ocean's angry billows roll,
When tempest tossed they cannot rest,

They foam in wild and raging shoals;
Once all was calm and quite inert,
Now upward from beneath it rolls,
In columns foul of mire and dirt.

Evil speaking, backbiting and evil surmising, defaming and villifying, were resorted to as means of self defense and promotion and exaltation, in the honor that cometh from man, while that wisdom which is from above, was turned out of doors, with its pleasant fruits and lovely companions; that which is earthly sensual and develish, and entered with its imps and inmates, where was envying and strife, confusion, and every evil work. The vile practice villainy; the base contemned the honorable, and the child and the youth behaved himself proudly against the aged.

How different this from the Bible rule: "Thou shalt rise up before the hoary head, and honor the face of the old man, and fear they God," Lev. XIX, 32. With this the practice and example of Elihu of old well agreed, Job XXXII, 6, 7, who said, "I am young, and ye are very old, wherefore I was afraid and durst not show my opinion; I said days should speak, and a multitude of years should teach wisdom." But in those latter days of improvement, the aged often had to wait for the young first to give their opinion, and display their superior knowledge and marvelous precocity, then the old might, with caution, modestly venture a supposition, in their vulgar way, in the presence of refined, scientific young Americans. And sometimes when the venerable preceptor attempted to maintain primitive order—

By his old fogy means and rules,
Now obsolete in homes and schools,
He learned from Bible mouth sublime,
And youth held dagger's polished tongue,
That he was quite behind the time,
Among those brave and rising young.

A state of things now existed much like that described and lamented over by Isaiah, III, 12, "As for my people, children are their oppressors, and women rule over them. O my people, they that lead thee cause thee to err and destroy the way of thy paths." The principle was encouraged and cherished to render evil for evil, and to bear injury, reproach or insult from no man, but to resent and revenge it. This was brave, manly and noble; but when reviled or unkindly treated, to pass it by without reviling again, resenting or raising a storm about it, was too ignoble, mean spirited and effeminate.

Parents who had the best interest of their offspring at heart, and felt deeply concerned for their future welfare, and were more anxious to promote their spiritual and eternal interests than to secure for them an honorable station in the world, or a popular position in fashionable society, found it almost impossible to stem the tide of surrounding influence, and train them up according to Bible precept, so as to secure that good part, in comparison with which all earthly good dwindles into insignificance and is lost sight of, as a taper blown out in midnight darkness. But, alas! how few families were to be found in these perilous times, where the parents were heartily united in their plans and efforts for the defense of the truth, with an eye single to the glory of God, practicing according to his word, with their faces Zionward and their backs upon the world, with the resolution of Joshua of old: "Let others do as they may, as for me and my house, we will serve the Lord." How few had faith and moral courage enough thus to go forward, confiding in the power and faithfulness of God to accomplish his work and fulfill his promises of good by the means of his own appointment, without the fashionable policy of this enlightened age of serving both God and mammon and of transgressing the laws of God that they may conform to the fashions and customs of the world, that they may thereby increase their popularity and ability for effecting good among the people. "Them that honor me I will honor, and they that despise me shall be lightly esteemed, saith the Lord." I Sam. II, 30.

Though Christ has said, "If any man love me he will keep my words; and ye are my friends if ye do whatsoever I command you. If any man love wife or children more than me he is not with me." Yet how few among those who professed to be the friends of God, but who like Eli of old, despised or set so lightly by the commandments of God that they honored the desires and lusts of themselves and of their children by complying with their requisitions in preference to those of God; and would encourage and gratify a child or a companion in that which they knew to be contrary to and forbidden by the law of God.

When parents differed in their notion of religion and government, the ones whose system was most in accordance with the flesh, the world and the devil, had greatly the advantage in influence, as it corresponded and co-operated with human depravity, and was therefore a most dangerous enemy to the spirit and interests of the rising generation.

This state of things might well be compared to a person rowing his way against wind and tide with a companion on board unfriendly to his progress, who though much his inferior in strength, yet can easily by an occasional opposing stroke, prevent his progress, turn him aside or thrust him backward so as to defeat his purpose.

Such was the unhappy lot of many who were unequally yoked in the marriage relation with unbelievers or non-professors, and consequently spent their best days and energies in toil and anxious care raising children, many of whom, as St. Peter says, were as natural brute beasts, made to be taken and destroyed, who should utterly perish in their own corruption. Upon whom the sayings of the Lord by the mouth of his prophets, is as fully accomplished as they were upon the Jews of old: "Because you have forgotten me, I also will forget your children."

Although the state of Zion was such that one, when looking at the dark side of the case, might be led to feel someteing like the prophet did when, in reply to the question, "What doest thou here? and he said: Israel have forsaken thy covenant and thrown down thine altars, slain thy prophets, &c., but as there was then seven thousand in Israel whe had not bowed their knees to nor kissed Baal, so perhaps there were that many who were exceptions to the general state of things in those latter days, for there were still a few faithful ministers, who, Elijah like, were bold defenders of the truth, who stood up for the old paths and faithfully instructed the people, and solemnly warning, reproving, rebuking, admonishing, and entreating them with long suffering patience, telling them of the lowering clouds of wrath that were gathering and thicking over their heads, soon to break forth in bolts and storms of judgment and destruction upon a guilty, God-forgetting, Sabbath-profaning, covenant-breaking, gospel-slighting, Christ-rejecting, Heaven-daring, God-provoking, Hell-deserving people, who, knowing the judgments of God against those who do such things, not only do the same, but have pleasure in those who do them. The watchmen saw the sword coming and gave the alarm, but they took no warnings, but many made light of it and went their own way; and those preachers seemed to them as Lot did to his doomed sons-in-law: as one that mocked, and they were fast preparing for that to be true concerning them that was said of the Jews at the time of their subjugation by the Chaldeans and captivity to Babylon, II Chr., XXXVI, 16. But they mocked the messengers of God, despised his word and misused his prophets, till the wrath of God rose against his people till there was no remedy.

It was too true with regard to a majority, that they would not receive instruction, that they hated reproof, and though often reproved were obstinately determined on their own chosen way. Their true character and the consequence of which is clearly set forth in the scriptures: He that refuseth instruction despiseth his own own soul. He that hateth reproof is brutish. He that being often reproved hardeneth his neck, shall suddenly be destroyed, and that without remedy. All they that hate me love death. When all the workers of iniquity flourish, it is that they shall be destroyed forever.

These things clearly showed to those whose eyes were open, what was stored in reserve for the future, and they felt the force and applicability of the prophet's words: "Be ye not as your fathers to whom the former prophets cried, saying, thus saith the Lord of hosts: turn ye now from your evil ways and from your evil doings. But they did not hearken unto me, saith the Lord. Your fathers, where are they? and the prophets, do they live forever? But my words and my statutes which I commanded my servants the prophets, did they not take hold on your fathers?

The fountains of society were corrupted, and the foundations of family, civil and religious government and order were out of place. Opposite extremes were resorted to in their policy for training and governing the young, perhaps equally pernicious to happiness and good order in society. According to one plan all was to be effected by kindness, flattery, persuasion, indulging, hiring and perhaps threatening or promising what was seldom executed or fulfilled. Some thought that using the rod was useless and injurious; that it was unnatural, unfeeling and cruel in parents, and only calculated to produce hatred, disrespect and unkind feelings in children toward parents, and that it was a kind of government only suited to a barbarous, uncivilized people, slaves and brute beasts, but entirely unworthy of this highly refined age of superior light and improvement, and of the highest grade and most noble of the human race, destined soon to give law and order to all nations, break every oppressive yoke of tyranny and despotism, undo all the heavy burdens and let all the oppressed go free, proclaiming a jubilee of liberty and freedom to all the inhabitants of the earth, which will be glad tidings of great joy to all people but the Neros.

A great portion of those trained according to this plan were in the habit of setting lightly by the authority, wishes and rules of their parents, only so far as they corresponded with their own inclinations. And generally going unpunished for their disobedience, and without threats being executed upon them, the disposition to disregard law, and evade and escape from justice, was fostered in them from infancy, and having practiced successfully in family and civil government, they were encouraged to think that God also was such an one as themselves, and that they would have their own way, and, finally, in some way, would escape his justice; and hence were disposed neither to fear God nor regard man. Children growing up under the habit of being indulged and waited on a great deal, often carry the effects of it with them through the whole course of their business in the world, and down to the latest period of life. When they go to school, the teacher must do almost everything for them, and, in religion, the preacher and the church must do all; and in all cases, they must do as they please.

Another class seeing the error and evil of a child being left to itself, and that it is a scripture truth, that it brings its mother to shame, and also that the Bible directs us to use the rod, and promises a blessing upon its use, they attempt to keep everything in its place by brute force and by tyrannical coercion, without the persuasive influence of reason and kindness, and all is crushed into order and formal submission, alike to the dictates of passion and of lawful authority, without manifesting any regard to the pleasure of the subject. This is indeed calculated to produce opposition, and rebellion and prejudice against all strict laws, human or divine, as being arbitrary and unkind; and hence a strong disposition arises to throw off the yoke and disregard them whenever they think they can.

The safest and best plan for training the rising generation, to secure their happiness and welfare, and the way aimed at by a few lies between these extremes, and is that which has been prescribed by Him who has given to us our existence with all our capacities, and fully comprehends the whole of our complicated and mysterious nature, and all the sources and springs of thought and action, and know exactly what is best suited to the case, and has given us the rules that have been dictated by infinite knowledge, wisdom, skill and goodness, and far transcends anything that human skill can devise, God has given us the laws and counsels of his word, which he has required us to lay up in our hearts and to practice them in our lives, and dilligently teach the love and practice of them to our children, and talk of them when we sit in the house, when we walk by the way, when we lie down and when we rise up, &c. Not that we should be thus continually employed in word, but enough to have them thoroughly fixed in the mind of the young, and we should so order our conduct and the disposition of our hearts, that by the temper and spirit of our minds and uniform course in life, we may manifest and act out what the law enjoins, and thus teach it at all times and under all circumstances, not only by word but by actions which speak louder than words.

As the All-wise Creator, who perfectly understands our nature, well knew that these in themselves would be insufficient to secure the proper training of children and the best interests of man, he has plainly taught us this; and also the proper means to be used, and what will be the result, and also some of the consequences of their neglect, that none are by nature disposed to do good. "We all go astray from the womb. Foolishness is bound up in the heart of a child, but the rod of correction shall drive it from him." Prov. XXII, 15, XXIX, 16. The rod and reproof give wisdom; but a child left to himself bringeth its mother to shame, 17. Correct thy son and he shall give thee rest; yea, he shall give delight unto thy soul, XIX, 19. Chasten thy son while there is hope, and let not thy soul spare for his crying, (to his destruction or cause him to die,) XXIII, 12, 14. Withhold not correction from the child, for if thou beatest him with the rod he shall not die. Thou shalt beat him with the rod and shalt deliver his soul from hell, XIII. He that spareth the rod hateth his son, but he that loveth him chasteneth him betimes. Train up a child in the way he should go, and when he is old he will not depart from it. The lip of truth shall be established forever but a lying tongue is but for a moment."

Doubtless it was to this old and divinely inspired rule of instruction and government, and the necessity of its being carried out under any dispensation, the apostle had reference when he enjoined it upon parents to train up their children in the nurture and admonition of the Lord. And again, not to provoke them to wrath, (as I understand, by harsh, tyrannical, or unreasonable treatment,) lest they become discouraged. He also plainly infers, Heb. XII, 6, 11, that it was fully understood that children who had lawful parents and were properly cared for were trained by this rule, and if they were not, were neglected and treated as bastards. If this old rule was generally attended to, how changed would be the condition of the world.

If parents, with an eye to the high responsibility of their station, the glory of God, and the good of his creatures, holding the reigns of government with a steady hand, proceeding with unshaken firmness and decision, acting from principle, with the best interests of their children at heart, and would go forward in the discharge of their duty, firm to this purpose, immovable by wrath, sympathy or affection, first learning to be governed and to govern themselves, and then would teach those divine precepts to their children, by which under God they are bound to govern themselves and their children, so long as they are under their care and legal control and representation, and would faithfully explain to them the wisdom, goodness and necessity of those precepts which they are bound to obey themselves, and cannot and dare not disobey them, nor suffer their children to do so with offending God and exposing both to his righteous displeasure, and thus teach them, and that it is their duty and interest to obey and please so great and good a being as he is, and that if they will not they must be punished. When parents thus faithfully instruct their children in their duty to God, parents and others, with the happy effects of obedience set forth on one hand, and the miserable consequences of disobedience on the other; if, then, a child proves wayward and disobedient, they, firm to their post and faithful to their trust, let it know that there is no escape from punishment, but transgression and disobedience must have their recompense, and when they inflict punishment let the child see that it is intended for its good, and to do their own duty, and not because it is any satisfaction to them, and that they are grieved and distressed at its wickedness, and that it is painful to them to have to punish their child, so much so they would gladly receive it themselves, if it would have the necessary effect on the child, (which certainly is true, at least with all christian parents who have tender feeling for their children.)

Blind, perverted human nature, with all its stubbornness, can hardly withstand such persuasive arguments. Parents who thus proceed in the exercise of government, humbly trusting to God to bless the means of his own appointment and make them effectual in accomplishing the desired object is not likely to be disappointed. Many who have thus gone forth with bleeding hearts, weeping and bearing precious seeds, have doubtless come again rejoicing, bringing their sheaves with them, of a glorious harvest of the peaceable fruits of obedience unto life, temporal and spiritual.

Would parents thus perform their duties they would greatly add to, and promote the interest and happiness of thempelves and their children, their neighborhood, the church, nation and the world of mankind, "God's would be the glory, man's the boundless bliss."

Perhaps it is proper and necessary here to notice some of the organizations of men that considerably affected the condition of the church. And here I take the position that God, who is possessed of all possible perfections, both natural and moral, to an indefinite degree, has given us in his word a perfect system of religion and morality, and a better system of civil and religious government, and better calculated to secure good order, peace, happiness and prosperity in the human family, than anything that they can devise apart from it. The great object of law and government is to prevent evil, redress and punish wrong, promote, defend, and reward the good. Therefore that which is most efficient in the accomplishment of this end is the wisest and best system. Now who that has any experience in human nature does not know that if the Bible rules of teaching and governing were carried out, and the penalty or violated laws was inflicted to the letter, whether unto death, or to an eye for an eye, &c. The number of deaths from murder, and the execution of criminals, and the damages and suffering from violence, and the punishment inflicted upon transgressors would be ten times less than it is, and the state of things would be ten times better than what now is. If that system had been properly attended to we would have had none of the trouble of the war with which we are now burdened and destroyed; as a matter of course, all the calamity, carnage and blood, distress of body and of mind, loss of life and property, is traceable to the violation and neglect of those rules, and those who have acted and thought so are chargeable with it all.

We are prone to two great evils : first to forsake the rules God has given us, and then presumptuously attempt to devise something of our own, superior to these, and better calculated to promote our interests; hence the isms and schisms, associations and organizations for which there is neither precept nor precedent in the scriptures.

We have had different organizations of this kind, each with a mouth speaking great things for its self, and promising to do great things for the people. Most of them have had good enough connected with them to give them the appearance of an angel of light, at least in the eyes of many, such as free masons, odd fellows, sons of temperance and good templars; all of which hold forth some object, lawful and good in itself, as that which is to be effected by them, and better than could be effected without them. God has not in his word, so far as I know, ever authorized or said anything good, but always evil of such orders or organizations as these, whose terms of membership and the signs by which they are known to themselves, is a secret known only to themselves; and their meetings are required to be held, and their business transacted with and among themselves, to the exclusion of all others ; an organization and practice never justifiable where the right and privilege of performing every duty to God and man is enjoyed, and only where these are interfered with by the laws and authorities that exist.

What is light ? That by which knowledge is gained through the organ of sight; and, figuratively, all correct knowledge of things is called light; darkness is its absence, in a natural sense; and so, in a moral sense, that which conceals or prevents knowledge is called darkness.

Again, what is meant by the unfruitful works of darkness, and the things done in secret, of which it is a shame to speak, but the doings of organizations of such a kind? Yet we find societies in these last days formed after the pattern and example, to some extent, of these ancient mysteries of iniquity, who make tall pretensions to being the authors of a vast amount of moral, civil and religious improvement; and they had become so popular in the south, that most of the leading men, both in church and State, belonged to them. Even the preachers, of most religious denominations belonged to them, and it was thought by many to be necessary to enable a man to have influence, and it was argued, that if there was any harm in them, so many good people would not stay in them.

But if that position were necessarily true, the same argument would prove many other anti-scriptural practices to be harmless: such as the fashions and vanities of the world, the lusts of the flesh and the pride of life. Covetousness, unfair dealings, oppression, breaking the marriage relation without the consent of the parties, and preventing the fulfilling of the marriage contract, preparing the way for and encouraging unlawful conduct, persons rejecting the proper training of those committed to their charge; and, in short, anything and everything that can be practised among men, so as to make it fashionable and popular, and, on that account, highly esteemed among men, though abominable in the sight of God,

Claims were made by professed ministers of the Gospel, and belonging to some of those orders, especially the sons of temperence; that the sons of temperance were doing more for the good of the world than the church was. Some went so far as to assert that they were doing, and had done more good than all the churches and preachers had done. It was generally admitted that if the church had done its duty there would have been no use of such societies; but inasmuch as the church had been so corrupt, and had departed so far from the performance of her duty, such organizations had become necessary, which, by the by, was an ac-

—4

knowledgement of the truth of our position: that the system of Divine appointment is sufficient to meet the necessities of the human family, if attended to according to divine appointment; therefore, the failure is chargeable to men and not to the system; and, of course, when people become corrupt, and subject themselves to calamity and evil, by departing from those divinely appointed rules, or by corrupting and incorporating human invention and traditions with them, the wisest and best course to pursue is to bring the people back to the good old way, to trust to God and his own authorized and instituted means. He that does so shall be called a restorer of paths to walk in; but they that trust to the devices of their own hearts and the inventions of men, and turn the attention of men to these things, and encourage them to trust to them, instead of that ordained of God, are such as the prophet describes when he says: "They that lead them cause them to err and destroy the way of thy paths." "He that trusteth to his own heart is a fool" Prov. Deut. XXVII, 18, "Cursed be he that maketh the blind to wander out of the way. Cursed be the man that trusteth to man and maketh flesh his arm, whose heart departeth from the living God." Presumptuous are they, proud blasphemers against God. The more a thing that is useless can be made to resemble that which is useful and valuable, the more likely are people to be imposed upon by such counterfeits, and to be subjected to all the evils to which they are thereby made liable.

A vast amount of time, labor and money has been used to keep up and furnish these organizations; and though I admit that, as Tertullus said to Felix, very worthy deeds in themselves have been done by their providence, yet, I doubt not, they have got more credit for them, from themselves and the world than is their just due, or than they will ever get from the Judge of all the earth, who may say of them as he did of some of old, who sought the admiration and honor that comes from men, more than the approbation of God: "Verily, they have their reward." Had they devoted as much time, money and labor to religious and benevolent purposes, in strict accordance with divinely instituted rules, the good resulting therefrom would have been as much greater as divine wisdom exceeds human skill.

So far as I know, it is a rule generally with these organizations, which are denominated secret, because the signification of their signs and the transactions of their business are concealed from other people, that they are bound to befriend their own fraternity, in preference to and beyond what they are required to do to any others. This feature, in some orders, has been held forth as an inducement to others to unite with their order. "If ye love them that love you, and do good to them that do good to you, and give to them from whom ye expect as much again, what thank have ye? Do good to all men, especially to those who are of the household of faith," is the apostolic rule. But if they have a member who makes no pretensions to piety, and his life plainly shows that he has no right to such pretense, yet they are bound to protect and defend him in preference to the most devoted saint or christian upon earth who does not belong to their order.

Again, the theory has been handed out that they were doing much in preventing political discord and division; that they were the cement of the nation, the adhesive plaster of the Union, and were chiefly to be depended upon for its preservation. Had they lived under such an administration as that of Nebuchadnezzer, long before this they would have been promoted to Haman's hights, thence to survey the happy fruits of their salutary institutions, in the enviable scenes of our divided country. Where is their boasting, then, when the whole nation is involved in the horrors of a desolating war, introduced by thousands of traitors in our midst? while we have reason to believe a large majority belong to some organization for concocting schemes and devices in secret.

The very existence of such an organization is a reproach and slander upon any just, good and equitable government, for it is equivalent to the declaration that the government where they exist, does not allow to, or protect its subjects in the possession of the free use and enjoyment of what God has given them a right to, which is all that any one is justifiable in desiring, claiming or asking for himself or any one else. So, then, the existence of, or desire for such institutions, shows that those who do such things think the government under which they live does not guarantee to them the free enjoyment of their divinely authorized rights, or they are possessed of a disposition to obtain for themselves what they have no right to, and, of course, at the expense of right and justice.

I honestly believe it to be very impolitic in any government to permit any organization, civil or religious, to exist within it, with the privilege of holding meetings for the transacting of business, which is a secret known only to themselves; or, in other words,, any society or organization of a kind that secrecy is essential to its existence, perpetuation and prosperity.

To make the best of it we can, supposing all the societies we have named to be free from all unjust and impure designs, and therefore such institutions ought to be tolerated in the government, this policy is like that of a person who has certain domestic animals, which may go into his fields and stores without damaging his fruit and goods, and he therefore thinks he ought to, and does, leave a pass-way for them to go through at pleasure, without his knowledge, but in so doing, leaves those things exposed to the ravages of all other animals of equal and less size, whose disposition is to tear up and destroy his fruits and goods. Who that has any considerable knowledge of the state of things in our country at this time, but is aware that the privileges and practices of secret associations have had much to do in bringing it about? Yet they have caused excitement in their time, and promised great things to the people, engrossed the mind and choked out the word and rendered it unfruitful.

The following were among the things that had their influence upon the state of morality and religion : horse racing, circuses, exhibitions of men and beasts, feats of art, comic songs and clownish deeds, scenes of vanity and vice, with which the minds of many were corrupted. Great things were pretended to be accomplished by phrenological knowledge, mesmerism, and spirit-rapping, all of which had a fame for mystery, which held the public mind spell bound for a time, and diverted the mind from matters of more vital importance.

At the same time, political party policy, prejudice, ambitious strife and jealousy, were on the march with increasing speed. But upon this subject I wish to be brief, as in these things I participated sparingly, and assumed the name of no political faction—more of my time was devoted to theological, than to political studies. I never made a political speech, nor subscribed for a political newspaper, (though often furnished with more than I was willing to take time to read), nor ever left my home to listen to political speeches, though often heard them when my business required my presence where they were delivered.

The country was now divided into political sects, each of which had their newspaper organs, by which they proclaimed and trumpeted abroad their high and noble objects and the superior excellency of their own party leaders and party policy, and claimed that the public interest was greatly dependant on them and their success, while they brought huge charges of dark deeds of dishonesty, unfair and false representations against their opponents, whom they represent as being destitute of veracity, and guilty of condescending to mean, low and groveling deeds, for the accomplishment of base and selfish ends, endeavoring to thrust others down, that they and their party might thereby rise at the unjust expense of good men's characters and interests, who were greatly superior to themselves.

Each party made high claims to philanthropy and patriotism, but made most hellish meals of good men's names. Loud and long were their discourses about the rights and liberties and interests of the common people, for the protection of which they professed to feel great concern and much zeal. But it was a fact, too notorious not to be understood by the commonest mind with a little observatien and experience, that this zeal for the rights and interests of the people in too many instances was like that manifested by Judas of old in behalf of the poor, which, indeed was not that he cared for the poor, but because he was a thief and had the bag and what was put therein. So they wanted the fat offices, and they would compass sea and land to accomplish their object; so that there was reason to believe that in those charges brought against each other, there was often more truth than fiction; and it might almost be said in truth that the political press was a licensed organ of slander, infamy and reproach, often burdened and teeming with the polluting and demoralizing fruit of human depravity.

> Such are the winds that often blow,
>   And such the streams that onward glide,
> The woful state of nations show,
>   While on the downward sweeping tide,
> Mid loud, and harsh, and jargon crash,
>   And ever fulminating roar,
> And rubbish vile and worthless trash
>   Obstructs from sight both sky and shore,

Polluted imps with brazen face,
  Strut forth in pride to make pretense
Of right to fill each worthy place,
  Though void of grace and common sense.
Deception, pride and self conceit,
  Presumption, vain and shallow show,
Sits high at ease in honor's seat—
  Sense, truth and grace must stand below.
And demons dark in robes of light,
  Around them shed a bright display,
True saints of God shined out of sight,
  As tapers hid in light of day.
The humble poor are out of sight,
  The meek and lowly just and true,
The church's hope, the Lord's delight,
  The slighted, chastened, chosen few,
Their humble homes a calm retreat,
  A place that suits my taste full well,
Where kindred spirits love to meet,
  With whom the Lord delights to dwell.
Away from public strife and noise,
  Are scenes where thought delights to dwell.
A pleasant wife and girls and boys,
  A father's heart with pleasure swell;
The young ones taught to fear the Lord,
  The hoary head to honor well;
Instructed by the holy word,
  True wisdom's guide, the way from hell;
They learn to love and praise the Lord,
  Devote themselves to God in youth,
And study well his sacred word,
  And walk in ways of peace and truth.
To God they well may render praise,
  For that to which he makes them heirs;
On earth he gives them many days,
  Then God, and Christ, and all is theirs.

How different this from the generality of those leaders and aspirants after worldly wealth and stations of power, honor and profit in a sinful nation, laden with iniquity, where they are contending and striving after the fading and transitory vanities of time—

  Which were as painted, airy bubbles
    That down Time's rapid current shined,
  And broke and left in endless troubles,
    The void, deluded, worldly mind.

CHAPTER II.

CONDITION OF THE SLAVES AND SLAVERY IN THE SOUTH.

It is reasonable to suppose that one coming from a southern part of the Southern Confederacy, would be expected to give some particular statements with regard to the condition of the slaves of that country—their treatment, natural capacity, &c., the views and feelings of the people generally with regard to the propriety and good policy of the institution.

The condition of the negro, like that of domestic beasts, differed very much according to the different kinds of owners; as almost all kinds of men owned them, they had various kinds of treatment, according to the dispositions of the owners, and that which was sanctioned by popular custom.

Where the country was poor, and divided into small possessions, the slaves not numerous and few owned by one person, as a general thing their condition was more comfortable; they enjoyed more liberties, and were more intelligent and happy. But, on the other hand, in proportion as a country was rich and its inhabitants wealthy, negroes numerous, and many were owned by one person, their condition in every respect was generally worse. They were kept under closer restrictions, subject to heavier exactions, and the whites participated less in regular manual labor, less sympathy was shown the servant and less attachment to the master. There were some very humane, good hearted men, who regarded the temporal and spiritual interests of their servants, and tried to promote their comfort and welfare, both of soul and body, furnishing them with a competency of food and clothing, and instructing them so far as the laws of the land would allow. And some were taught to read, though the law did not allow it.

Some, perhaps, were treated in all respects as well as the

circumstances of such a relation would admit of; and doubtless many of this class of slaveholders were doing better than many who were not masters, only because they could not be such, and were condemning and finding fault with others for that of which they were innocent only because they were not able to be guilty, though their deceitful hearts might not think so.

Again, there were those who cared no more for the comfort of their negroes than they did for their beasts, and showed less kindness and respect to them than they did to their favorite dogs. Many, by their mistreatment, had their capacity for usefulness much diminished; some were rendered useless, and some died of mistreatment; some while receiving punishment, and others of the effects afterward. A condition between the two extremes described, was the one occupied by the largest portion of the negroes in the south. When they were not overworked, and were furnished with plenty of food and clothing, though of a coarse kind and roughly prepared, they appeared to be the happiest people in the country. There was a marked difference between their appearance, strength, and capacity for business, and that of those whose dry and faded looking skin, thin features, languid, downcast countenance, and sluggish appearance, plainly showed the lack of the property that supports animal nature, and imparts vitality and vigor to his movements.

Of late years, numbers of them were furnished with good houses, much better than those of many of the poor white population; but how they were furnished within, I cannot tell, for I have no recollection of being or seeing inside of one for the space of twenty years, so as to know what was there. When I was on the muster list, liable to serve in parole companies, whose business was to go round to the negro houses, within the bounds alotted to their inspection or vigilance operations, and see that the darkies were all in their proper places. But I must acknowledge that what I then saw made a deep, lasting and unfavorable impression upon my mind with regard to the institution of slavery; and if what I then saw was anything like a good specimen of the condition of the negroes generally, in the slave states, theirs was a condition that no one who was not destitute of sympathy and compassion could survey without their feelings being stirred within them, on account of that which none but an infidel could contemplate without fearful forebodings of woful calamity awaiting the nation; especially when they thought of the character of that God, from whose all-seeing eye no one of those things were concealed.

The time has been when many of the slaves were taught to read, and some were well educated, and there were well educated, respectable and able ministers among them; and also private members of society, who met and participated with the white brethren in conducting social worship. They often had meetings of their own; the services were conducted by men of color, and the whites went to, or stayed away from them, as they chose. But such things of late years were of very rare occurence. Negroes were not allowed to assemble and conduct religious worship without white persons present.

As to the general opinion of the people of all classes in regard to the propriety of the institution of slavery, until within a few years, with few exceptions, it was believed to be wrong and a great national sin, which would at some time, if not done away, subject the nation to great calamities. Many there were who lamented the evil and dreaded the consequences; but inasmuch as it was fashionable, honorable and profitable, and one could not easily maintain their position in society without participating in it, they justified themselves from the consideration that they were not guilty of bringing them into bondage; and if they were here some would have them, and they might as well, perhaps better have them as some other who would not treat them as well. And so they persuaded themselves that, upon the whole, it was quite a clever, respectable and worthy deed.

At times there was uneasiness in the minds of many with regard to the impropriety of holding them in bondage, and a dread of the consequences; some liberated and sent them to Liberia; others lived in continual dread of them. Yet, for a number of years, the disposition to liberate and colonize them appeared to be diminishing, and people appeared to be growing more determined upon the perpetuation and extension of slavery, fastening more strongly the fetters upon the slave. Laws were enacted to prevent negroes from being taught to read and write; and also to prevent anything from being said in public speeches, or by the press, against the institution; but all were allowed to bring forth arguments, both in public and in private, in its favor and defense. Books were written upon the subject, some professing to prove from scripture that slavery is a divine institution, and, of course, right. Some would prove it by phrenology, that the negro was capacitated only for a servile position in society; that they were incapable of scientific attainments and of self government, &c. Some pretended to prove by anatomy that they were not the same grade, or species of being, as the white race. Some professed to prove from the scriptures that the African, or black race, were descended from Canaan, and were the subjects of the curse pronounced upon him by Noah, for the misconduct of Ham; others, that they were the descendants of Ham, and inherited their color and the degradation of their race from him; that his name signified black or brown; and his *name* and *color* were both given him because of his mistreatment of his father.

Of course, the judgment in part preceded the crime. Some said they were not descended from Adam, although they acknowledged that they were a race of human beings. Others, again, represented them as being nothing more than brutes, having neither *soul* nor *future* existence. They were frequently spoken of, as being very little superior to a baboon, in point of intellect and intelligence, and, in a great measure, destitute of any quality that is lovely, noble and elevating in the human character. Everything mean, base and degrading, was compared to a negro. This was a common mode of comparison.

Although they were considered to be so polluted and degraded as to be disgusting and repugnant to every feeling of refinement and decency, so as to be unworthy to be associated with white people; yet there were those offering for the highest civil offices, and among what was called the higher class, who could condescend to equal themselves with those degraded creatures in secret, and that in unfaithfulness to, and violation of the marriage contract.

I have been told by persons from different southern states, who professed to have a good chance to know, that they believed there were very few men raised during the last thirty years, in the bounds of their knowledge, who were not guilty of this degrading kind of equalization; and it is a well known fact that, about many of the popular towns, a great amount of the children of servants were of mixed complexion, and many of them as fair as most of the free;

and some of them much whiter than many who owned slaves.

Again, there were persons holding many slaves, who had a decent church for their blacks to assemble in, where they had them preached to, and the scriptures read and expounded to them, and they catechised upon what was read to them. Some had the scriptures read to them so frequently, that they had a better knowledge of what was taught in them, than many white persons; and some appeared to be much attached to, and have a great reverence for their owners, and acknowledged that they were well treated, and were thankful for their happy lot.

But the reverse was true of others. While some allowed them to attend preaching on week days, the same as they did themselves, others did not encourage them even to go on Sabbath. Many who were members of churches, and in good standing, exacted all their ordinary labors from their negroes on fast days, which were common with some denominations.

Many professed to give to their negroes the same diet they used themselves, though this, I think, was not often the case. I once had business at a house where this was the professed rule in the family, and I thought it as likely to be so there as at most places. There, several negroes with clubs were chasing a hog. Said I, "What are you going to do with the hog?" "Kill um," was the reply. "What are you going to kill him for?" "To eat." I learned that the hog had been given to them by their master, to be butchered for themselves; which they did, and made use of it. Had any one offered such a beast to him, for such a purpose, he no doubt would have been greatly insulted.

It was a favorite theory that the negro is an inferior race, of small intellect, and not capable of much mental improvement or scientific attainments; yet it was argued that it was unsafe to educate them, for education and knowledge gives power, and if they were educated, they could not be kept in bondage; and, therefore, to protect the peace and safety of the country against outrage from those black savages, it was policy to enact laws to prevent their education, which was a tacit acknowledgement that the negro is naturally so near their equal, that if they gave him an equal chance with themselves, they could not keep him below them.

That there are many negroes who are naturalty smarter

than their masters, is a fact so notorious to any southern man of common sense and observation, that he well knows that any one who denies it, is either simple, ignorant or dishonest. By the labor of such, many have been raised, supported and furnished with the necessaries and luxuries of life, and all necessary advantages for mental culture, improvement and qualification for usefulness; and, with all, have never arrived at anything worthy of notice. Some of whom have all their lives been an expense, and, by their own labor, have never paid for their nourishment; while there was many a servant who possessed a bright intellect, capable of such development and improvement, as would enable them to perform the duties of the highest offices in a manner that would do honor to any man, of any color.

Yet, with all these natural advantages, they were compelled to spend their days in servile labor for those who were much their inferiors in capacity. Thus they were fettered down in obscurity, under the infamous epithets heaped upon their unfortunate race. Yet, in despite of all the embarrassing circumstances with which they were surrounded, their superior talents would sometimes break forth like sunbeams through the parting cloud. In some of their discourses, such was the eloquence, clearness and force with which they expressed themselves upon subjects of the greatest importance, that honest white men, of common capacities, were heard to exclaim, "It makes me feel mighty little to hear that nigger preach."

Some are ready to say such are rare cases. Just about as rare, in proportion to their number and circumstances, as what is called self made men among white people, who, by their own energetic efforts, unaided by others, have, from obscurity and nothing, risen to stations of distinction, influence and honor. If God has endowed them with capacities for performing so much, how criminal in his sight must those be, who, for their own pecuniary interests, keep them fettered down in ignorance, under circumstances calculated to break down and crush out every noble principle of their nature, deprived, in many instances, of everything calculated to inspire and encourage ambition for, and a sense of personal honor, honesty and claims for respectability, to increase and perpetuate degradation, foster and cherish all manner of corruption and licentiousness that human depravity can instigate.

The laws of the land authorized the breaking up and tearing assunder of the tenderest ties, nearest and dearest and most consoling relationships that God has instituted or the human family enjoyed, for promoting their comfort and welfare, while sojourning in this world of trouble and sorrow, and for securing the better interests in eternity. Such things have often been done at the pleasure of the owners to accomplish their selfish purposes and plans of pecuniary interest, to the deep mortification, distress and depression of spirit to the slaves, who were represented as being without natural affection, having a woolly head, flat nose, thick lips, sleek, black skin, and a strong odor! A picture, from the thought of which it would seem that refinement and good taste would almost shrink and recoil. Yet all this could be surmounted, and those creatures, so disgusting, revolting and repugnant to their refined feelings, could be made one flesh with the noble, refined and highest grade of human beings.

In the scripture it is said: "He that oppresseth the poor reproacheth his Maker," and that God has made of one blood all nations, to dwell on the earth, and that he is no respecter of persons, but, in every nation, he that feareth him and worketh righteousness is accepted of him.

The Ethiopians are recognized in scripture as being of the nations of the earth; and as God has not only given the leopard his spots, but the negro his complexion, features and form; then, whoever reproaches and mistreats him on account of these things, reproaches his Maker, and is guilty of blaspheming the character of Him who is the author of that, on account of which he claims the right to treat him differently from all other people.

Of late years, people professing to be christians, the light of the world and the salt of the earth, have had the audacity to charge the Almighty Ruler and Judge of all the earth, who will do right, with being the Author of the institution that authorizes such conduct toward fellow beings.

As this is done in the last and only christian and civilized nation under heaven, that tolerates this institution, and is one that makes claims to superior light, improvements, &c., is it strange that the Almighty should arise to vindicate the honor and dignity of his character against the reproach of such a charge, from such a source, that he should ride forth in the garments of vengeance, to purify with judgment, smiting them with madness and blindness, and sending them strong delusion, leaving them to go mad upon their idols, and become the weapons of his indignation, the instruments in his hands of executing his righteous judgments upon themselves and the idol of their choice, which they have chosen to their own destruction, and confusion of their own faces, and to their own shame and reproach among the nations, in whose eyes the Lord shall be exalted, when they shall hear of his judgments and fear. In that day when the haughtiness of man shall be humbled, and the loftiness of men shall be brought low, the Lord alone shall be exalted.

Some would gravely tell us that the *color* and *bondage* of the negro race, is the curse pronounced upon Ham, for his sin in the case of his intoxicated father. Without condescending to controvert such a theory, I shall just remark, that if all crimes of equal magnitude had been visited upon the perpetrator and his postority in a similar way, I think by this time there would have been neither white nor free people in the world; and if the degree of human criminality is to be shown by the blackness of their complexion, I am constrained to think that some of the white people of the present age are destined at some time to be the blackest creatures in the universe, unless there are others, who, owing to superior capacities and opportunities, can commit greater crimes; for if they are not sinners above all men that dwell upon the earth, surely, it is because they have not capacity to be so.

The civil laws, though generally good, were often badly executed, and the guilty often went unpunished, and the innocent, especially if pure and virtuous, frequently suffered wrong without redress, while perpetrators of the greatest crimes and outrages, if wealthy, could generally go unpunished. This was a strong temptation to the injured party to resort to unlawful and violent means for redress. The knife and the pistol were the weapons used by the combatants of the wealthier class, who were generally well provided with such means of defense. To fight without weapons, was thought to be a vulgar and ungentlemanly game, only fit for negroes and underlings, who, also, were too fashionable and polite to condescend to old style.

  Fashions, like manners, from courts descend,
  And what the great begin the vulgar end:

Though to carry, send or accept a challenge to fight a duel, was a crime, punishable by law, yet it was resorted to as the most brave and honorable mode of deciding differences between contending parties. Challenges were not only given and accepted, duels fought and the actors screened from the law, but, if I am not mistaken, some such characters were candidates for, and promoted to the highest offices of honor and trust that a State can confer on a citizen.

Means honest and dishonest were resorted to, publicly and privately, by office seekers and their understrappers; their hands were full of Bibles and their mouths with falsehoods. The public and private treat bought many an unworthy vote, and perhaps put many a wretch into high office, who was more worthy of a gallows or penitentiary.

While it was admitted on all hands that negroes should not be allowed to vote, there were scores of white men who could neither read nor write, and who were more ignorant in the most important matters pertaining to both Christ and State than many a good man's negro; and doubtless many who were not so ignorant sold their votes, or cast them in a certain way, for the indulgence of a beastly appetite, or to aid in promoting a member of some oath bound fraternity to office.

Among the hungry swarms of office seekers that roamed around and infested those southern regions, was a class of people called preachers, professing to be ministers of the gospel, some of whom not only claim to be ministers of the gospel, but members of the only true church, regularly descended from the apostles, and who alone have legal church authority, and her ministers the only authorized persons to administer the ordinances of the church, and whose privilege it is to say to all others Stand off, for I am more holy than thou. Yet, for the sake of securing their promotion to stations of honor and profit, they could condescend to furnish intoxicating drinks in order to obtain the aid of a low, grovelling, unprincipled class of people, who loved the intoxicating bowl better than their family or country. And if some of those high pretenders were not grossly misrepresented, they could participate freely in this luxury themselves to the animation of their own animal nature.

The language of the evangelical prophet might well be used in reference to a people where such things exist: "The whole head is sick and the heart is faint; from sole of the foot to crown of the head there is no soundness in them, but wounds and bruises and putrifying sores."

CHAPTER III.

PERSONAL CONCERNS AND INCIDENTS.

Having lived in what is now called Lownds county, Miss., (with the exception of three months) from June, A. D. 1820, to 1848 or 1849, and having settled myself with a family, and also having engaged in the gospel ministry—to this I was desirous to devote the remainder of my days—but as there were a number of different denominations, and more preachers than had much ground to occupy, I felt it my duty to look out for another field of labor, and after visiting different sections of country, I arranged a chain of appointments in Fayette and Marion counties, in Alabama, where I labored some time in hopes of usefulness; but the distance from home was so great, that it was attended with great inconvenience and loss of time—as in those regions back from the advantages of market, there was less of the vanity and extravagance of the pride of life, than prevailed in localities more convenient to trade, and as there were good winter and summer ranges, and I could live at much less expense and be more convenient to my appointments—I rented out my farm in Mississippi and spent about two years in Alabama, when I returned to my former residence, after having undergone many hardships, and past through many discouraging circumstances : in clearing land, building houses, attending appointments far and near, teaching school at a distance from home, and from that to which all have to be subjected who will live Godly in Christ Jesus.

When I returned things were much deranged and out of repair, and much labor required which had to be done with my own hands, which left little opportunity for study or ministerial labors. I was thus left without means to go to another country to obtain a situation adapted to my case.

In view of so much of my past life being spent apparently

to little profit, and the period of my life to which I was then advanced, and no visible door of usefulness being open before me, and everything hanging in a state of suspense as to what course I should pursue, I felt as if I was unnerved, overwhelmed in darkness, and all my energies paralyzed. I felt the ravages of disease and premature old age preying upon my vitals, and, by those circumstances, as with a fire shut up in my bones.

I was fettered and gagged, while vanity and wickedness were stalking abroad with gigantic strides, and error and the seeds of corruption and iniquity were being sown broadcast over the land, and were springing up and ripening for an awful harvest of fearful calamity and woful destruction; in view of which my feelings were made to correspond with the language of the Psalmist: "Oh, my God, my soul is cast down within me." "My feet were almost gone; my steps had well nigh slipped;" not so much because I was envious of the prosperity of the wicked, as because they were permitted to prosper and enjoy so many blessings so long without their iniquities being visited with tokens of Divine displeasure, while the unfortunate, humble and self-denying were so often afflicted, downtrodden, disregarded, forgotten, and subjected to so many trials and troubles. I was almost ready to conclude that I was an ultraist, and had understood the laws of God to be more strict than he had intended them, (and that surely I had chastened myself and undergone self-denial and privation in vain,) and therefore it was that he was dealing so gently and kindly with those whom I had thought were so guilty in the sight of His just and holy law. Yet I could not be persuaded that the day of their calamity was not rapidly approaching.

Though I am no friend to superstition, and to giving interpretations to every foolish dream, yet I have had dreams and impressions and have noticed occurrences that appeared so indicative of something of serious importance, that I could not forget them.

Previous to, during, and some time after my sojourn in Alabama, my slumbers were often rendered uncomfortable by distressing visions: one in particular was repeated I know not how often, in which I saw two armies approaching each other at the place of mortal conflict, and about to engage in the dreadful work, while part of my relations were in one and part in the other, and as I knew of no reasonable cause of difference, or anything to justify such a course, I was anxious to dissuade them from their purpose, which, I felt, would soon result in the loss of life; but was saved from witnessing the reality, except on one occasion, which was some years previous, and was a most shocking sight.

In a dream, I saw two opposing armies coming in close contact, when, by stratagem, effected through the instrumentality of dogs, by which those with whom I was allied, diverted the attention of the others from them, and, at the same moment, making a sudden dash on them, put the last one to the ground with the bayonet, which, to me was a most shocking sight. And what made it more distressing to me was, my oldest son, who was then a small boy, appeared to enjoy it as a scene of pleasant amusement.

Another vision comes to view: A large and furious rattlesnake made its appearance in my father' house, passing over the floor half erect, sounding the alarm with his rattle, and producing much trouble and alarm to those present, the particulars of which I omit. I remarked to a brother shortly after, that if there was anything indicated by dreams, there was reason to fear that the old enemy was going to get into business in our church or family connection. Not long after I learned that things were then in progress that afterward involved the whole church and family connection in trouble, and subjected many of them to deep distress and sore trials, the affects of which are visibly and sensibly felt to the present day, though it began more than a dozen years ago, and many of those concerned in and affected thereby, are now in their graves, whither those that remain are rapidly tending, while the adversary is still going at large, seeking whom he may devour.

> And death and hell close at his heels,
> On thousands prey at daily meals.

Again, unusual discords in church music, were accompanied with the painful impression that they were premonitions of trouble in the church, and discord among brethren, all of which I afterwards witnessed to my heart's sorrow and deep mortification.

Again, on a certain occasion, as I arrived at, or before noon at a place, which had been dear to me on account of the manifestations of the Divine presence there enjoyed in former days, there I saw bats flying around in open sunshine, when the following suggestions presented themselves to my mind : Perhaps the time is at hand when the deeds of darkness, which have generally been done only in secret, or in a sly and cautious manner, out of shame of being seen or known by decent society, would be practiced boldly and shamelessly before all classes. Whether those suggestions were correct or not, those acquainted with what has since transpired there may decide.

So strong were the impressions of a certain kind, at the time of the death of several friends of which I was ignorant at the time, that I was lead to say to some one present, that if what I experienced had any signification, we would be apt to hear of some of our friends dying about that time, which proved to be really so. Whether such things were accidental, or the effect of a supernatural influence, my readers may judge.

On the 4th of July, previous to a presidential election, not long after my return from Alabama, I went to Columbus on business, but as there was a public dinner and speaking on hand, the business houses were all shut but one, into which I went, but not finding the article I wished to obtain, I remained there till the people returned from the celebration. Several persons being there, they soon began to interrogate me with regard to my politics, and the way I was going to vote. Upon this subject I said little; and not wishing to have anything to do with political controversy, I asked how Solomon's politics took with them there? One of them pertly replied that some of his politics took *very well* with them there. Understanding what they had reference to, I felt as if I had made an unfortunate blunder, and for a while said nothing more; but as they stopped in more decent bounds than I expected, I remarked to them that perhaps they had not understood what I had allusion to. I observed, "Solomon says : 'Righteousness exalteth a nation, but sin is a reproach to my people.'" Said I, "These are Solomon's politics, and they are mine. We have an old book of laws for the government and regulation of our conduct, and if we act according to their requirements, we have the almighty power and unchangeable promise of the sovereign Ruler of the universe, pledged for our protection and defense, and we will be an exalted, prosperous nation. But if we trample under foot and disregard those rules, we may hold as many political meetings, have as many great speeches, call as many councils to devise wise schemes of political policy as we please, all our devices, councils and schemes of human policy will be carried headlong, and we will all go to destruction together"

In the latter course they were rapidly tending, and with increased velocity, as time advanced, and the old passed from, and the young took the stage of action, with their claims to superior endowment and qualifications, to speed the march of improvement in this progressive age of light and knowledge; while corruption of morals and forgetfulness of God were generally on the increase. Politics, worldly pleasure, wealth and power, were the all absorbing topics.

Gain was preferred to godliness and sometimes passed for it, though obtained by ungodly means. The smooth faced stripling, especially if he had enjoyed the high privilege of being nursed by a negress, could dictate to the man of hoary locks and many years, how he should vote, and think, and act, in all important matters, and could say a great deal about the right and the wrong among political parties and opinions.

As time passed on, we heard of Whig, Democrat, Republican and Know-Nothing, all praised and extolled, all reproached and villified, all justified and all condemned, by their advocates and opposers. The institution of African slavery became a great matter, that ought not to be spoken against, and much was said in its defense and justification, to relieve the minds of those who doubted its propriety and feared the consequences that would result from it. Pro-slavery men maintained that the negroes in America were in their proper sphere, and the only one for which they were capacitated, and that those in America were in a better condition than the same number of their race were anywhere else, now, or ever had been; that they were more enlightened and comfortably provided for, and hence it was a great blessing to the negro race. And, according to this theory, it was quite a righteous, worthy and commendable thing to participate in, encourage, defend, support and extend the institution. Yet they acknowledged that it was ruining the white race, making them effeminate and worthless.

An ultra pro-slavery candidate for the state legislature, while in my house previous to the last election, previous to the rebellion, speaking upon this subject, remarked, that it was impossible to train a family to business as they ought to be, where they have many servants, for if parents told their sons or daughters to do anything, they would tell a servant to do it, rather than do it themselves. He then told an anecdote, illustrating the ignorance of some southern ladies of the process by which their daily comforts and luxuries of life were provided. He had heard of one who asked her mother which of the cows gave the buttermilk!

It is a fact that ought to be clear to the understanding of every person of common sense and observation, who has much knowledge of human nature, that, provided it could be fully proved and established from divine authority, that the negro ought to be in bondage to the white people, and of course it was the duty of some whites to have them If, then, the owning of them would subject the possessor to disadvantages in the way of property, honor, ease and influence in the world, as great as the advantages it has given them in these respects, it would hold good as a general rule that those who have been the most anxious to own them would be the lost people that would be persuaded that they were the persons whose duty it was to own them. So that it is plain that the origin of the happy lot of slaves in America, so far as man has been concerned, has been owing to his supreme selfishness; and as to the benefit they have been to the blacks, for this they have their reward; and as to the blessing derived to the African race, through the institution of slavery in America, it is not so much attributable to their good will to the African, as to the fact that, as God makes the wrath of man to praise Him, and the remainder of wrath He will restrain—so He has made their pride and covetousness to praise Him, and has so overruled men's selfish purposes as to make them instrumental in accomplishing His benevolent designs. And while they are ready to say in the boasting language of Nebuchadnezzar of old: "Have I not done it by the might of my power and for the glory of my majesty?" He who has made all things for himself, even the wicked for the day of evil, is ruling in the armies of Heaven, and doing his pleasure among the inhabitants of the earth, who are fulfilling his purposes without meaning it so.

About this time I was led to remark to my family that the institution of slavery I thought was very near its end, that people were given over to blindness and madness, whereby they would hasten its destruction.

We had now arrived at the border of the mighty vortex of a bloody judgment by secession, and the smoke from the pit was darkening the air, and a great dust being raised about, making and breaking, proposing and rejecting conditions of compromise between free and slaveholding states, the rights of Congress in territorial governments, and much was said about John Brown and his negro riot in Virginia, and abolitionists instigating insurrection of negroes. The honorable congressmen were strewing the southern states with their speeches in Congress, in defense of southern rights.

I need not say much about the favorite policy of the leading men of the south, the part acted by their delegates to the Baltimore convention. Their object in so doing, which is well known to all intelligent persons, was a pretext for the course they afterward pursued. But the minds of the people were not prepared for participating in such a policy. But when Yancey's secession scheme began to be published through the country, so far as I know it was thought by the people generally, to be a shocking exhibition of the highest degree of madness and folly.

I somehow heard about this time, that there was a boast or threat made by some that there was a secret organization at work, that would, at some not far distant period, make a demonstration that would surprise the people. And no great marvel, for this was the sanctified means of this age of light, for the accomplishment of those professedly the best and most noble enterprises. And unquestionably, the policy of the principal leaders was to prepare a way for, and precipitate the peoole into the measure of secession; and, for this purpose, newspapers and public speeches must teem with false and exagerated representations of northern people, and of their wrong and unlawful deeds and designs against the south, and then get up an excitement and state of alarm among the ignorant and jealous hearted southern people, as if they were then suffering great and unreasonable wrongs from northern people, and were in great danger of being opposed and robbed of their rights by them.

Breckenridge and Bell were the only candidates for president worthy of respectable notice, where I was acquainted. Whether it was because Lincoln was called a black Republican, or from some other cause, it was no uncommon report that he was a negro or mixed blood, and I know not how many believed that it was so. As to Hamlin, it was a certainty that he was of the negro kind—

> It was a fact exceeding plain
> That one he was of cursed seed,
> Bearing the mark of Adam's Cain,
> Or that of Noah's Hamish breed.

A number of public dinners were given by the Bell and Breckinridge parties, the former claiming to be for the Union, the latter for seceding, each of which had their far-famed speakers, and great demonstrations were made, and a vast amount of time and money's worth was spent at those meetings.

After this course of things had begun, as I was one day returning from Columbus, I was overtaken by a Presbyterian minister with whom I had long been acquainted. He had that day been attending one of those political meetings, where he had for the first time heard secession openly advocated in public speeches, and appeared very much disquieted at such conduct. He also told me of a Union, or Bell meeting that was soon to come off, and requested me to give my brother (a minister of long standing) notice of it; and invited me to attend. I did not agree to do so, but asked if he did not see that those who kept away from such places were nearly all the rational, dispassionate men we had amongst us? He said, it really looked so, but things had got to such a pass that all ought to go, and requested me to attend.

Said I, "You wish me to attend and go mad like the rest of them, do you? I think people would do better for themselves and the country if they would take those men who were going round making exciting speeches, and hang them or put them in the penitentiary." He said it would have been well, he supposed, if Yancey had been hanged.

But the excitement was pressed forward till it appeared that people were by multitudes given over to the greatest madness and blindness to their own welfare, and they had gotten so far ahead that before the election came off, a call was made, and some volunteers were obtained for the express purpose of going to Washington to prevent Lincoln, if elected, from taking the Presidency.

It was said to be a prevailing notion among the negroes, that if Lincoln was elected they would be free, and that in some instances they had become quite insolent, telling their owners that when Lincoln was elected, they then would be as free as they were. And we had startling accounts of the detection of horrid insurrectionary plots among the negroes. It was reported, and perhaps correctly, that the negroes were frequently holding night meetings, the object of which was concealed from the whites. While these things were scared at and spoken against as being dangerous to the people, I was tempted to treat some of the advocates of secret socities as Elijah did the prophets of Baal, inasmuch as they represented them as being good and necessary institutions, and denied that there was anything wrong in the principle, or anything in them that had the appearance of evil or justified suspicion, or that had a tendency to evil consequences. I could say to them, using their own language, that there was nothing harmful or dangerous in secret associations, and the whites had let their light so shine through their secret associations, that the negro, seeing their good works, had been induced to imitate their good example, by getting up something of a similar kind, for the accomplishment of some good purpose; and as "what the great begin the vulgar end," they ought to be allowed to enjoy the benefit of it, and to be encouraged in a good thing. But it was not generally conceded that negroes had any business with such societies, though according to the principles held forth in the Declaration of Independence, they are the only people in America whose circumstances would justify them in the institution of such organizations.

When the result of the election was known, many appeared greatly provoked, that an abolitionist was to be our president. Some were declaring that they never would live under a president that negroes had elected. On one occasion I ventured to remark that I supposed the speaker would as soon live under a president that good, free negroes had elected, as one that mean white people had elected. But it appeared that I was in the wrong place, and had made a mistake, for I was soon zealously assailed by southern devotees, and particularly by one, who was neither very white, intelligent, nor possessed very good morals, and whose place in God's account, I had no doubt, was far below that of a good negro, bond or free. But I understand he has long since fallen a victim upon the altar of free will offerings, a sacrifice in the service of the confederate faith. Some having Cainish countenances, accompanied with violent nervous excitement and passionate gestures were emphatically exclaiming, "The old scamp, he shall *never* take his seat at Washington!"

The people were sadly divided, some advocating and some opposing the policy of secession; the secessionists growing more rabid, assuming, overbearing and grasping after the reins of government. It was remarked by some Union men, that whenever a man turned in favor of the seceding party he lost all his reason, and a person might as well reason with a stump, as with him.

On one occasion, before I was aware of the malignant, stage to which the excitement had progressed in the minds of the people, while in a store house in the town of Columbus, where, for the sake of showing a decent respect to one, who had some claims to human shape, but had lost his hearing, and then appeared to be acting under the influence of beefsteak madness, I had to stand and listen to a long and acrimonious story of grievous and insufferable wrongs, that southern people were being subjected to by the northern policy. When I was relieved from him, the proprietor stepped forward and asked me if I could receive the other man's views. I said I could not. He then gave another detail of grievous wrongs and consequent hard times, and said that unless we took measures to prevent it there was worse coming. He then asked me what I thought of it— and I was not aware that it was then unsafe for a man to express his sentiments honestly, when asked to do so. I tried to comply with his request, and as I had lately heard something of what was up, and my feelings were considerably stirred, I expressed myself to the following effect: If the people go on with their plans for protection and defense, they will pull down upon their own heads the very thing they are trying to prevent; and, instead of having good reason for complaining of oppression and hard times, the worst of all with us, is that we have more than we have a heart to make good use of. We have no just sense of the worth of what we enjoy, and what it cost our forefathers to secure it to us, and by the abuse of these good things, and their improper use in the course we are now pursuing, we are revelling, as it were, in the blood of our fathers.

Only look around and view the prosperity of the country, see how rapidly it is improving, and people are accumulating wealth, so as to be able to indulge in a high degree of luxury and extravagance, so that many of them in one year can, and do spend more mony for fashionable and fancy articles, and in the indulgeance of acquired appetites and habits, than their forefathers did in a whole lifetime, and yet we are murmuring and complaining of hard times and oppression. In view of these things, I feel that if justice was let loose upon us, it would sweep such a generation to destruction from the face of the earth. Now, sir, what do you think of it? In a more subdued tone of voice he replied that there was too much truth in what I had said, and that we did not appreciate our blessings as we ought: that we were a highly favored people, and greatly blessed with full barns and stores. Said I, not quite all of this just now, for we have been visited by droughts, and blights that have cut short the fruit of our labor, and we have been threatened with famine, and believed our wickedness had been the cause of it. What do you think of that? He said he did not think so, but, according to his observation, the wickedest men generally fared as well, if not better, than any; and he kept on with a long routine of sayings upon the subject, without giving any opportunity for a reply till he had to wait on a customer. I waited for him to return and pursue his subject, but he remained silent.

After silently looking him in the face for some time, I said I was waiting to hear him out, to see the applicability of what he had to say upon the subject. He said he had not time to spend talking upon the subject, and he supposed I had not either. I said I never pushed myself into such discussions, but when I took hold of a subject I wished to go through with it. Said he, I know you are a modest man and I hope we will not fall out about it. As he was anxious to get rid of the subject it was never mentioned by us again, though I often saw him after they had begun to reap the fruits of which they had been sowing, and thought he recollected and felt the truth of what I had said to him.

Great anxiety and disquietude pervaded the minds of all classes of people, and vigorous efforts were made by the fire-eaters, to get the slave states to withdraw from the Union, especially the gulf states, for if they could get a peaceable secession there were as many states as they wanted, for they said if the border states went with them, in the course of fifty or sixty years, which was a short period in the history of a nation, they would want to be free states, and the same battle would have to be fought again, and they would prefer being without them, unless they had to fight for their independence. In that case they would need their assistance to whip the Yankees, though they talked loudly of a peaceable secession. But they said if they could not get it peaceably, if it should ever come to a fight, the Yankees would get badly whipped, for one Southron could whip some said two, some five, some ten, and some twenty Northern men; and, if I have not forgotten, some were claiming the promise that "one should chase a thousand, and two put ten thousand to flight," for the Yankees were anything but good, honest, noble and brave men.

It was the soldiers from Southern States, they said, that did the fighting in Texas and Mexico, and achieved all the brilliant victories on the frontier, by which the new territories were acquired, from which treacherous Yankees had been scheming to exclude Southern rights; and by the aid of stolen and runaway negroes, have elected a black Abolitionist for President, who had pledged himself to his party to do all he could to destroy slavery in America, and whose grand object would be to abolish slavery in the Southern State, take their servants from and equalize them with, and make them work like negroes.

Shall they do it, said they; Heaven forbid! No; they may kill us, but they cannot make slaves of us; we will die before we will be servants. God has given us these servants, and in his word has authorized and recognized the relation of master and servant, and pointed out their relative duties, and He will not let them accomplish their cruel, unjust and wicked designs against a righteous, innocent and noble-hearted people; but will subject them to a shocking defeat, and fearful overthrow, to their astonishment and confusion, and to the deliverance and exaltation of the right.

As the dissolution of the Union was the great object to be obtained, and difficult to effect, owing to the strong Union feeling that still remained and prevailed amo g all classes of intelligent people, and as, according to the principles of Democracy, the right of government is in the people, and the majority must rule, the impending crisis was that of independent State sovereignty, over which, it was said, the Federal Government has no Constitutional right to exercise coercive authority or control, and this was the vessel rigged up by fork-tongued, red-mouthed fire-eaters to glide out of the Union on, and to have a claim to having proceeded according to Democratic principles.

The voice of the citizens of the States was called for, which was to be exposed by their votes for Union and anti-Union delegates, who were oppointed to meet in State conventions, where it was agreed to be decided according to the majority of the votes whether they would remain in or go out of the Union.

The election was held, and, as I understood, many knew nothing of it till it was past, and in some places they were not represented at all, and in others—as they were not quite awake to what was in progress—failed to attend.

Again, where it was fully understood, there were many Union men, nearly no Union votes were given, and the only reason I heard assigned for it was that they were afraid of the opposing party. And thus, in some instances, a majority of votes was obtained by a minority of those who had a right to vote, and where a decided majority was for the Union the opposition party managed it so as to force the ordinance of secession upon the State, and all the while were making a great clamor against coercion.

Were all the seceded States to tell the whole truth with regard to the means by which that end was accomplished, it would set the matter forth in the light in which it ought to be seen. But when a State was claimed to have seceded, many who had previously been Union men, and believed secession wrong, yet as the State was claimed to have seceded they then appeared to feel bound to go with it, and it became a popular saying: "I am for my country, right or wrong," and there is no sense in one opposing everybody.

Now three unclean spirits, like frogs, were leaping and croaking all over the Southern States, from the mouth of the beast that had a foot like a bear, (the institution of African slavery,) and of the dragon, (Satanic policy, which by falsehood and misrepresentation perverts righteous laws and governments to corrupt and selfish purposes,) and of the false prophet, (the class of people that were crying *peace! peace!* and predicting a peaceable secession, and were offering to bet that there would be no war, nor a gun fired; to pay the expense of the war; to drink all the blood that would be shed in the contest, etc.

*—6

The pestiferous gas of these filthy creatures was issuing from not only farm yards, lanes and fence corners, but from the stump and stand in the grove, field and fair ground, and pulpit in the church, and from the cellar, street corners, court house and city hall, till soon the time came when the man who would not openly acknowledge that he was in for the southern confederacy, and was for his country, right or wrong, was no patriot, but a tory or mean submissionist, and did well to be cautious in his words.

To defend the confederacy, armies must be raised, to withstand Yankee invasion and to compel the federals to relinquish their pretended claims to places and property in the Confederate States. Great honors were to be obtained, and lasting renown inherited by the noble and brave boys who would give their voluntary services in a cause identical with that in which our forefathers fought under the immoraal Washinton, and achieved the glorious boon of American liberty and free government; and it was understood that those who would not avail themselves of the advantage of securing to themselves such high honors, if needed, would have to go into the service by the dishonorable process of drafting, which no noble-hearted American would do himself the discredit to wait for. It was said that in some instances, when the men were slow to volunteer, the ladies offered their hoops to them, which was thought to be a cutting reproof.

There was now a great military spirit in the land. Boys were drilling, and ladies were reported to be drilling at some places, and to be good at a mark with a pistol. A certain class of the wealthy were indulging the remark that there was plenty of scamps in the country to do all the fighting, and all they would want would be a suit of clothes, blanket and gun.

Again, it was said, the wool hats and cotton breeches would do the fighting. Though at first many thought it would be quite a pleasure spree, and a number pitched into it of the wealthy class; but many who failed to get into office, were like a cat pitching into the fire after a mouse, and, if there was any chance, they soon pitched out again. In some instances, owing to a misunderstanding or disagreement between the officers and soldiers, companies broke up and returned home, after they had been transported to some distant point, and an indisposition to going into the service was on the increase, and, in some places, there were strong symptoms of resistance. Great policy had to be used, much flattering teasing, persuading and cautious threatening, and even shaming, villifying and blackguarding were resorted to to get people into the ranks. A bounty, good treatment, high honors and immortal renown, and the good graces of all the fair, were to be conferred upon the manly, patriotic volunteers, who would have the chosing of their own officers, and have their acquaintances for messmates; while the skulking, cowardly, odious Union men, or tories, who would have to be dragged into their country's service, by draft and conscription, would get no bounty, and would be sent to fill up broken regiments among strangers, where they would be little cared for. Such were to be laughed and hissed at, and their families subjected to odium and reproach, that would stick to them so as not to be wiped off for many generations.

> And thus they compassed land and water,
> And marshaled hosts for death and slaughter.

Some were in favor of fighting under a black flag, and of neither giving nor taking quarter.

> Victory or death was what they said
> A cloud of black rose o'er their head,
> And thunders shook the earth below,
> And streams to ponds of blood did flow.
>
> The wail of death spread far around,
> And mangled heaps lay on the ground;
> In tones of thunder justice spoke,
> Amid the scene of blood and smoke.
>
> As by a flood they now are swept,
> Who long have been as those who slept,
> Mid dangers thick in open day,
> Unconscious passed the time away.
>
> To them the call was made again:
> Return, return, ye sons of men,
> For ye are all as tender grass,
> On which the blighting winds may pass,
>
> Your glory all, as flowers bright,
> One hour shines, next out of sight;
> The howling winds went sweeping o'er,
> They where they were are seen no more.

Thus man with all his pride and boast,
Must fall and die, give up the ghost;
As him no longer here we see,
The question now is, Where is he?

The one he chose while here he staid,
With him his future home is made;
Just as to Christ he gave his heart,
Or chose in sin to have his part.

CHAPTER IV.

INCIDENTS ILLUSTRATING THE VIEWS, FEELINGS AND DIS-
POSITION OF SOUTHERN PEOPLE IN THE MORNING
OF THE CONFEDERACY.

On the day on which the news of the seceding of South Carolina was received in Mississippi, I and my companion went to Columbus. When we were drawing near to town, we heard the oft repeated roar of cannon, and when entering the borders of the city, the bells were ringing and people were running as if fire was raging in the city, and perhaps some thought it was.

On arriving at a house where I frequently sold country produce, our beast had participated so much in the excitement, that it was thought to be unsafe to proceed till the excitement would pass away. The lady of the house was in the yard, apparently in an ecstacy of joy. Being asked what all that noise meant, she exclaimed, "South Carolina has seceded, and Mississippi will be next! We are going to have *good* times," and seemed as if she felt too light to touch the earth for exceeding joy, as if a long looked for jubilee at last was come. But, to me, it was like the funeral knell of a parent, for South Carolina was the land of my nativity. I felt awfully, as if in sight of death and destruction, and solemn as if judgment and eternity had been in view. The horrors of war, with its distress and calamity, blood and carnage, in all their woful aspects, almost as in a picture of living fire, blazed before my imagination, so that I could not well contain myself, and I remarked to the rejoicing lady, that we felt very differently on the subject, and if they kept on with that matter, soon many pale faces would be seen; and said I, "It is our pride and wickedness that is bringing these things upon us." She claimed for herself that she was not proud. I replied, that I should not pretend to justify myself, for I believed we were all guilty, and I would acknowledge that I was worse than anyone ought to be, and I thought I would be willing to give her whole estate if I had it, to be able truthfully, to say of myself what she had said of herself—"I am not proud." She perhaps admitted that we all do wrong, but said she was above doing a mean act, and she knew that she had that much pride.

She then began violently to criminate northern people, laying all the blame upon them. I replied, "We need not go so far to look for wrongs, when they are so plenty nearer home. If we would get things all right at home, we would not have so much to complain of abroad, and it would be easier to have them righted there."

Said she, "The north began it. They have been stealing our servants, and trying to keep us out of our rights; they have no right to meddle with our servants. We are told in the Bible, that there shall be servants, and servants of servants. The scriptures give rules for masters and servants to go by." Said I, "Very true; if we would only go according to them, all would be right." She said she believed there was a people that was *intended* for servants, and that it was right, that they ought to be servants.

Being asked who they were, she said a curse was pronounced upon *Ham*, and it was said, a servant of servants should he be to his brethren. She was told that was not in the Bible. She insisted that it was. I said: "The curse was pronounced upon Canaan, the *son* of Ham." I asked: "Who are his posterity? where are they now?" She thought they were the negro; I thought not, and gave reasons for my belief, and asked her to prove her position. This she did not attempt to do. Said I, "Perhaps you are one of them." She said she was not. Said I, "How do you know?" She said she did not think she was. Said I, "Prove that you are not, for perhaps you are; and if so, you ought to be a servant; and perhaps I ought to have you for my servant." This was not so palatable to her refined taste, as to do to others what she could not wish to have done to herself.

Some time after this, we had some conversation concerning the troubles in our country, and because I said the south were to blame, as well as the north, she said I ought not to be suffered to live there. I had been in the habit of furnishing her with many of her table refreshments, she then concluded to get her supplies elsewhere. Sometime I passed her by without calling, till we chanced to meet in town, when she lectured me for neglecting her, so I called on her again.

By this time several regiments of soldiers had been raised, and supplies had to be furnished them, and provisions were getting up to an uncommon price, so she blazed out at me for asking high prices. Said I, "Good times have come now, and you can afford to pay high prices." She gave me to understand that she as fully as ever, believed theirs to be a good cause, and that the Good One would give them the victory at last. I was aware that it was useless, as well as unsafe, to spend many words on the subject.

On another occasion, while sitting in my wagon conversing with an old acquaintance, J—— B——, an officer in a vigilance committee in town, came upon me, interrupting our conversation. A letter had been written for him by my brother and sent to him in an envelope, bearing the representation of the hanging of John Brown. This had been shown, perhaps the day before, by the bearer at my house. Blair wished to know if the letter had been received which he had sent to my brother. I informed him it had. This, I think, was on Friday. He said my brother had desecrated the sacred desk with abolition, heretical, or perhaps infernal doctrines; had said a slaveholder could not be a christian, and if he did not answer him the next day, he would go the next Sabbath and hang him in his own pulpit. Said he to me, "*You sha' n't walk these streets—I'll hang the last one of you,* that hold such doctrines." How much more he said in a threatening way I cannot now distinctly recollect. As he could not hear, I did not try to converse with him, but let him take his course, till he was satisfied to quit and leave.

In the meantime my old acquaintances disappeared. When Blair was gone, as I did not take such treatment very kindly, I asked the merchants, before whose door this took place, who were witnesses to what had passed, why they suffered a person, who was peaceably attending to his own business, to be assailed in such a manner in their streets. They, looking as if they were alarmed, said they had no law there then. Said I, "If you do not approve it why do you suf-for it? On the same day I met with a brother of said Blair, previously postmaster, and a man of some respectability in that place, and asked of him an explanation of his brother's conduct. He attributed it to a communication received from Aberdeen, a town some twenty miles distant from Columbus. I remarked that it was a strange thing that people who had so long been acquainted with my brother, his doctrines and manner of preaching, should give credit to such reports. In the church of which he was pastor, a question to the following effect had been brought forward and discussed in *presbytery: "Is the practice of buying, selling and holding a fellow being in bondage, for the sake of gain, consistent with the rules that Christ gave his followers to be governed by?—which, by the vote of the presbytery, was decided in the negative, and was entered upon the church record, in connection with a resolution of presbytery, of about the following import: "Inasmuch as there is good evidence that there have been many christians of exemplary piety, and eminent ministers of the gospel, who possessed a high degree of the life and power of religion, and whose labors have been greatly blessed in the conversion of sinners, and to the edification of believers and the building up of the kingdom of Christ in the world, therefore the presbytery is of the opinion that being a slaveholder is not of itself a crime sufficient to exclude one from the church and the enjoyment of its ordinances."

This, however, was very mortifying to the feeling of many, and a rumor of it went into all the country round about and to many who were afar off, and perhaps assumed a hundred false and odious forms, very offensive and provoking to many. I said to Blair, if they were not satisfied as to his sentiments if they would go and search the church records, there they could learn for themselves, without any more trouble about it. He expressed his regret that he had not seen me sooner, and professed to have felt a regard for my brother, for he, himself, had been trained by parents of the same faith.

When our position in the government was spoken of I observed that we were acquainted with, and thought we understood and wished to obey the command, to be subject to the powers that be: that we had been allowed to think for ourselves and exercise our judgments, and enjoy our private

---

*Every church forms a presbytery.

opinions about matters. He gave me distinctly to understand that the people were not allowed to say anything against their confederacy. Thus I was growing in knowledge.

When I was passing where public speeches were being made, and heard the cheers given by the women, moving sensations thrilled through my whole system, produced by the suggestion, that, accompanying those sounds, which was that they were emblematical of outcries from calamity and distress, that would be heard throughout the country at a period not very distant in the future.

A short time before the attack on Fort Sumter, I was detained from home one night on business, I and the man of the house being out till after supper, while we were taking our meal the son was reading in a newspaper, just received, and when we went from supper, the son informed the father that the federals were making preparations to give up Fort Sumter. Said his father, " I knew all the time there would be no war, the northern people know better than to come here to fight. There has been nothing but quarrelling in Congress for several years, they have got separated now, perhaps we will have peace."

Said I, "You recollect that it is said, when they cry *peace, peace*, then shall come sudden destruction." The old lady remarked that she supposed it was better to separate than to have war. " Of course," said I, " if we can better the matter by it; but if we separate and have war too, we may not make much by the experiment. You know what is said of a house or a kingdom divided against itself. For my part, I see no grounds of hope for any lasting peace, till there is a reformation among the people, and they become more humble. In a short time after we heard of the taking of Fort Sumter.

After leaving Alabama and returning to my residence in Mississippi, I occasionally sent appointments and held meetings at a place where I had previously preached in Alabama, where I appeared to have won the confidence of the people, so as to be able to have much more influence with them than I could while living among them. I think in the last week in July, 1861, I visited that country, intending to hold a meeting of several days On getting into the neighborhood I learned that others had an appointment at the same time and place, that I had expected to occupy, and that on Friday, the day before, there was to be a time of public speaking, and a call for volunteers at a muster ground, where they were then holding a camp muster, and the candidates for the first confederate legislature and senate, were making ready their last speeches, as the election was to come off the next week. As nearly all my acquaintances from the hill country of Marion, Fayette, and all the region roundabout Sugar Creek, Luxpalile, and Bear Creek, and the inhaitants of the plain, and a great multitude from Yellow Creek were to be there, I concluded I also would go with them. And lo, a great mulitude of wagons, chariots, horses, mules and oxen, were there. A multitude of soldiers, captains, confederate officers in military array, drums and instruments of music. Old men with banners, and young men and boys; old wives and maidens, and a mixed multitude of women and children and many candidates.

Now, the names of the seven speaking candidates were these: The first Senator Coleman, a minister and chief ruler in the synagogue of hard shells, and Sugs, a teacher of science, Davis and McMullen, a minister and also a disciple of John Wesley, Logan, a minister of the Cumberland order and mighty in the doctrines of secession, and Stidem, whom the Union men had elected to the state convention, lest the deceivers of the people should persuade their rulers to secede, and one Brown, who was also called Cimbo, whose look was more stout than that of his fellows, like unto an Ethiopian of great stature; the same was mighty in gesture and demonstration of the power of pride, personal confidence and self esteem.

Much was said by several of those men concerning the great defeat of the Yankees in Virginia, (sometimes called Yankee's Run), and the great spoils that were taken. Some appeared to be quite jolly at their fanciful picture of *old Scott*, making his *gouty* legs *clatter* in his flight from the victorious confederates! The man who could tell the biggest tale upon the subject, and make it out to be an easy matter to whip the Yankees and have peace upon any terms in a short time, was the great man of the day. They were very urgent with the people to volunteer, and told those who had wives and children they need not make that any excuse for not volunteering, for their families would be well provided for, if they had to be away from them; and perhaps they would not have to go into the service at all, for peace would be made in thirty days, and perhaps in twenty, if they would all volunteer and let the north see that they were determined to have their independence.

Some of those speakers said the poor people thought they had no interest in the war, but they were sadly mistaken, for they were the people who were liable to the greatest misfortune; for if the Yankees gained their object the moneyed men would hold all the land, and the poor would be their tenants, as was the case in Europe, and even in some of the northern states of America, where the poor are worse off than the slaves of the south. They had a story made up of something intended to excite in every class of which the country was composed, a fear of damage to their several interests, and thus to give to each a portion in due season, to secure their assistance in the war.

They told the people that the Yankees intended to come to the sunny south, and if they had not been defeated and prevented from their purpose, by the south taking the stand against them that they had, their country would have b en taken from them; and they were *still* aiming to do it, and *would* do it, unless they were whipped and driven back. They said it was the object of those northern invaders to come and kill off the white men, take the land, free the negroes, and preserve the white women for the negroes and foreigners, whom they had hired to fight for them.

These things they told for honest, serious facts, in the presence of all the people, to persuade them to go with one accord into the war, as the only remedy against insufferable calamity and outrage, and many appeared to receive it for the truth; but I could not refrain from tears when I saw how those people were deceived among whom I had labored, and for whose welfare I had a tender regard, and whom I then viewed as sheep being lead to the slaughter. I then thought and spoke of it to my friends when I returned home, that they were probably then doing as did the Jews in the days of our Savior, when they said, if they let him thus alone, the Romans would come and take away their place and nation, when if they had followed his counsels it would have preserved the nation; but they pursued a course that subjected them to the thing they professed to be afraid of, and the scripture was fulfilled which says, "The fear of the wicked, it shall come upon him," and they, perhaps, will do likewise. I then thought the people, when they found out their mistake, would turn with fury upon their leaders.

As I was parting with one of my old acquaintances at the breaking up of the meeting, I said to him (who had the secession palsy), and about all that my feelings would permit me to say: "We have done that over which we shall weep when it is too late. Not many months had passed till one of his sons and several others of that section of country had fallen victims to the calamity of war, and were no more.

In the fall I formed a succession of appointments through a portion of Fayette and Marion counties, Ala., which I sometimes attended alone, and sometimes in company with a nephew, who sometimes went in my stead. By this time we had to hear the war spoken of on all occasions, and dissatisfaction and disaffection pervaded the whole country. Some companies of volunteers had been made up in these counties and had gone to Tuscumbia, but owing to some improper management, they broke up and most of the soldiers I think had returned home without being sworn into service. Some were blaming the officers and some the soldiers, who were charged with running away, and were deserters. Many by that time were tired of the business, and not disposed to return to the service, and different measures were taken to scare and persuade them back; and some were busying themselves about hunting them up, and were going around searching houses for those who were missing. This provoked the inhabitants till they were like hives of bees, whose lives had been rudely molested. Some of the soldierly women charging them bravely with the tongue, said that about the time they went to look under their beds, they would see sights and smell the patching.

A printed proclamation was shown around among the people in the name of the Governor, inviting the soldiers who had left to return to their companies, and they should enjoy the rights and privileges of volunteer soldiers, without any damage for the past, but such as failed to do so by or before a specified time, would be treated as deserters. Seeing people reading those papers at some of my appointments, for my own satisfaction, I asked if they had the Governor's signature to them, and was told they had. I afterwards learned that the opinion I then privately entertained was correct, and that the Governor was entirely ignorant of the document.

The requirement for conscripting all liable to military duty, between the ages of 18 and 35, was published not far from this time, but there were so many false reports that people neither knew nor believed much of what they heard.

Fall and spring passed away, times getting continually worse, notwithstanding the many favorable and encouraging reports of good success and a prospect of foreign interference in behalf of the confederacy. According to the most of the reports of battles, great slaughter was made of the enemy, with trifling loss to themselves; and when disasters were heard of, it was unpatriotic and censurable to give currency to the knowledge of the unwelcome fact. If a man was friendly to the Union, his credit and safety were best preserved by keeping that fact mostly to himself, for abolitionisis and Union men were two of the most odious and dangerous characters known of in the south.

Arrangements were next made to enroll all the male inhabitants between 35 and 50 years of age, and to organize them into companies for regular drilling, and to be in readiness for a draft, which was much looked for. People had volunteered and gone out of the country, till men were few, and, among poor people, the women, children, old men and invalids had to do the farming, and could not well on weak days take time to attend church. Under this discouraging state of things, I at one time had serious thoughts of giving up my appointments; but rather than do that I filled three or four appointments on Sabbath, and the others at night. Meetings were generally small and much disturbed by surrounding circumstances, which were continally growing worse.

In my travels I often passed the places where in times past they had had their political meetings and public dinners, and the visible signs still remained of the multitudes that had formerly attended them, and the question would not unusually arise, But where are they now? and where is all the profusion of luxuries in which they once could revel here? When the melancholy response that echoed from scenes of camp and mortal conflict was, that many had fallen upon the field of bloody contest, or of diseases in camp or hospital; others were sick and many living on half rations, while many of their families at home were in uncomfortable circumstances, and, being poorly furnished, were beginning to be in want of many of the necessaries of life.

Such was the state of things connected with the country through which I was travelling and laboring.

*—7

One gloomy, damp Sabbath morning, as I was on my way to fill an appointment after a vast amount of rain which fell the night and evening before, I called at a house to give notice of the miserable condition of a house that I had seen on the way. There I was asked if I was going to preach at the school house that day. I said I had an appointment there. The man of the house said I would not have many to hear me. I replied that the day was quite unfavorable. He said that they would not be there if it was a good day. I asked the reason. He replied that they said I was a Union man, and that if I ever preached in that house again they would burn it down. I replied I did not know how they found that out. It had been told through that country previous to this that I was an abolitionist, and I had the understanding that both reports started from the same place, so I made it in my way and called, as I supposed, at the fountain head, where I found an old lady and her daughter seated by the fireside, and as I was damp and chilly an invitation to a seat with them was readily accepted. The father and two sons were gone to the army, which was then at Corinth, if it had not moved south.

The old lady soon began to talk about the Union men, and to blame them with all the trouble and distress of the war. She said the infernal Yankees had got the railroad at Tuscumbia—she wished they were all in the bad place. If she had them she could cut their hearts out—she could cut their livers into hash meat. Said I, "You certainly know that according to the Bible such feelings are very wrong. If you really mean what you say, you have need to look out for yourself, lest if the Yankees go to the bad place, you should have your part with them." She said she knew it was wrong, but could not help it. She was so aggravated she could not govern herself. She said sometimes she was so sorry she felt like crying, and again she would get so mad she could not help thinking and saying bad things, and she was always either mad or sorry. I said if she would try in the right way, she would be enabled to do better; if she would commit herself as she ought to the control of the proper One, He would assist her in the proper control of herself. Said I, "It is an awful thing for people to be so full of hatred and animosity that they can desire and take pleasure in the misery and destruction of each other. If they cannot bear each other here, how can they bear to spend eternity together in the same place to which they are hurrying each other with all their might and fury. I talked with them upon the subject till their tears told the tale of grief upon their faces. The old lady said, if any of her family were killed or died in the war, she knew she would never see any more satisfaction in the world.

In the course of our conversation I remarked that I supposed that by some people in that country I was thought to be a bad fellow, and was called an abolitionist. They appeared to be ignorant of any such thing, as if it was all new to them. I said if they could tell me what it took to make an abolitionist, I could tell them whether I was one or not. They said they did not know. I said it was likely that was the case with many who were making a noise about it, and did not know what they were talking about. I told them some of the different views people had of the subject, all of which made abolitionists with some people and only a part with others. I then told them what my sentiments were, and said if that made an abolitionist they were welcome to tell every one they saw that I was that kind of an abolitionist. The old lady said if that made an abolitionist she was one too, and said worse things of slavery and slaveholders than I had any disposition to indulge in. So enough was said upon that subject.

I then turned to the subject of Union men, and said I would not go round the stump about it—I would not claim to be a thing when it was popular, and when it became unpopular deny it—when the vote was taken I voted for the Union, for I believed to divide would bring war and dreadful calamity, and I did not wish to have any part in bringing such things upon us; and if I did wrong it was ignorantly, with a good design, and was more to be pitied than blamed. But you see, said I, my views were right, and secession has brought war with all its calamities. She then broke out against the leaders in the South, and said more than I was disposed to say in that line. So my task there was done, and the fire quenched.

I remarked that it was time to go to the meeting house, and asked how many of them were going. They could not say, but thought it was early. I said I would go and be there in time, and if they came we would see each other again. They kindly invited me to return for dinner. So I went to my appointment, and, to my surprise, they were the first that got there after I arrived. But sad the story: at my next visit to that place, one month after, their seat was vacant, and I learned that one of the young men had died, and his father not being expected to live, the old lady had gone to see him, but I think he died before she got to see him.

    Uncertain all things here below ;
    From blessings great, sad troubles flow.

    This was the land of immersion,
    Where the tree of science was small ;
    The land of Southern coercion,
    Where the sons of Belial were tall.

 In the District where I resided the names were now enrolled, and as I was not past the age of fifty, my name was on the list. Notice was given that on a certain day we had to drill. This was one of the days when I had to be absent to fill my appointments. As I was going on that business, I was told that if I did not attend muster I would be fined, and have to pay five dollars. I told them my appointments were out, and I expected to fill them, and if they saw fit to fine me, they would have to do so.

 I doubted the legality of their procedure, but would have attended had not my appointments been out.

 They had their muster, and another was appointed. When it came on I attended, and asked what they were going to do with me for my previous failure, and told them I wished to comply with all legal requirements, unless I had good reason for failing. I also inquired after the authority for what they were doing, and after being referred from one to another till I had gone the round among their professed officers and leaders, it was a failure—the thing sought for could not be found.

 After the drill, which was mostly conducted by men from other localities, our officers acknowledged they had no proper commissions, and said they would have nothing more to do with it till they had proper authority. But they had got the people together, and had men there to make speeches to them and pursuade them to volunteer. We were promised something good from a refugee from Kentucky, said to be a Baptist minister. In his *good* speech he told us we need not object to fighting against the Northern people for fear of fighting our own people, for he said they were altogether a different people, that they were decendants of Roundheads and Puritans, and, if I have not forgotten, he called them vandals and barbarians, and charged them with many acts of savage cruelty and outrage against innocent and unoffending people, and with mistreatment and abuse of women, &c. He in one part of his speech warned us against the delusive notion that if the Federals got the government into their hands they would be more favorable to us for being Union men. "No;" he said, "they would treat us all alike."

In another part of his speech, while endeavoring to impress the people with a sense of how dreadful a thing it was to be subjugated—to what an ignominious, insufferably degraded condition they would be reduced—entirely under the despotic power of the Northern invaders, in a voice indicative of the highest degree of contempt, said, these *Union* men will be put in authority over you, and will hold all the offices of profit honor and power in the government.

> Lo! what a great horn! what wonders it said;
> In treason and scorn it flourished and spread;
> Behold the great ram from terror had fled;
> He acted a sham and cracked his own head.

> And yet with both hands, fury and ire
> He scatters the brands and cries out "Fire!"
> Thus onward they fly, wars transpire;
> With slander and lie—hope of the liar.

> They thought, furthermore to have the Gulf States;
> And up threw the stone that cracked their own pates;
> They never would quit what malice could aim;
> They opened a pit—were caught in the same.

> Their covetous wish they could not forget,
> But like silly fish went into the net;
> A fortune how great, the negroes to heir,
> They followed the bait, and entered the snare.

> They find, when too late, how much they mistook,
> In taking the bait they hung on the hook,
> And now they must find, with sorrow and cost,
> That they designed to own they have lost.

> This truth they will find, though man oft object,
> What wisdom designs that folly effects;
> From those evil things the wicked project,
> The Lord often brings to happy effect.

> The wrath of the vain to God shall give praise,
> And what doth remain at present he stays,
> With power and skill right onward they go,
> His plans to fulfill not meaning it so.

One day while in Columbus, I heard some conversation that passed among some men on the street, who were speaking in high terms of the sentiments of Brown, ex-Governor of Mississippi, who was represented as having said he would rather see the southern states sunk in oblivion than that they should return to the Union. "So would I," said one, "I would rather they were sunk to the bottom; yes, unless *hell* is a worse place than I think it is, I would rather *go there* than go back to the old Union."

I was informed that a popular Methodist preacher, with whom I was acquainted, had said that he would rather have every man, woman and child in the states slaughtered than that they should be conquered by the north.

When the popular charge was making against the federal government, that its object was to free the negro, if I expressed an opinion at all, it was that the government had no such design to meddle with the institution of slavery, if the south would behave themselves peaceably, but if they went to war, and it amounted to anything serious, the negro would be sure to come in, and it would end in the destruction of the institution. When we had reports of great victories in favor of the south, my opinion privately expressed was that the better their success in the beginning, the worse it would be in the end, the greater would be their damage and their ruin more intolerable and complete. If they had been defeated and had given up at the commencement, the loss would be comparatively trifling, whereas, if they were successful for a while, their loss would be incalculable at last.

The southen policy was often advocated and justified in my presence and in my own house, and it was claimed that so righteous and good a cause would secure the Divine favor for its protection, defense and ultimate success. I admitted it was possible they might have good reasons for what they were doing, that I knew nothing of; but unless they had, I honestly believed they were pursuing an unjustifiable course.

Owing to a misunderstanding, I and others on a certain occasion went to hear a sermon, as we supposed upon the fulfillment of prophesy, but it proved to be in reference to the duties of the people in matters pertaining to the condition of the country, and the existing war. The speaker brought many accusations of grievous things against the northern people. They had desecrated the pulpit with political sermons, and corrupted the gospel with abolition doctrines; but before he was through the leprosy had broken out in his pulpit, and the plague was raging in his discourse, and one thought that what he was doing for himself, he knew not then, but would find out hereafter.

> Though ill it did suit by chance or by guile,
> What those did pollute did this one defile;
> And this was the song whatever betide,
> If right or if wrong I am for my side.
>
> This clearly reveals what all ought to see,
> Who otherwise feels a tory must be.
> This rule will stand good as all must soon find,
> No patriot blood belongs to this kind.
>
> Such came from the mouth of many called good,
> Who dwelt in the south and called upon God.
> To Heaven they prayed with fervent address,
> The rebels to aid and crown with success.
>
> The wicked their wealth at pleasure enjoyed,
> By judgment to be forever destroyed,
> The wicked rule, the people mourn,
> Of wealth and peace they must be shorn.

Had they followed his advice in some respects, the condition of persons confined in southern prisons would have been a happy one compared with what it has been. At the close of his discourse a Methodist class leader lead in prayer and opened his mouth wide for the Confederacy, and appealed to the Lord that he knew the righteousness of their cause, and that peace was all that they wanted. He prayed for his enemies, that they might be sensible of their wrongs, be brought to repentance and to escape from an unjust and bloody war.

As I was going to attend an appointment in Alabama, I was overtaken by a young widow, who was full of zeal for southern rights, and soon introduced the most interesting topic of the day, and informed me that the news was that the French were about to break the blockade, that it would be done in twenty days, if it had not been done then. I re-

marked that as we had had so many reports of that kind, all
of which had proved to be false, if that were true we could
take no comfort from it till we realized the truth of it. The
thought seemed to irritate her feelings. She said she hoped
it was so, and began to abuse northern people for bringing
on such a war, the object of which, she said, was to take
the southern people's property from them; the negro was
all they were after. I told her I did not believe any such
doctrine; I believed the government had no design or wish
to meddle with their property, if they would behave as they
ought, nor could they be damaged if they had remained in
the government. She acknowledged that the south did
wrong in seceding, but they were in the war then and they
must fight out of it; that they must go through with it
right or wrong, and she thought we would gain the day;
that the Lord would be on onr side, and presumed that any
one who would not aid in the cause was no patriot.

After we had gone some distance, and she had occupied
nearly all the time, giving me a chance to say but a few
words, I at last said to her that I had listened to her some
time, and asked her to hear me a while. Said I, " I will
take the Bible for my guide in what I have to say, as the
best and safest source from which we can learn what true
patriotism is; and if you will attend to the instretions it
will teach you whether or not it is a woman's prerogative to
take the lead in public matters. The Lord has taught in his
word that we, and all things, were made by him and for him,
that our lives, all our enjoyments are dependent upon his
pleasure. His is the right to command and our duty is to
to obey. He has taught us our duty to him and to one another; has given us rules to regulate our conduct towards
our Maker and our fellow beings, under all circumstances
and in all the relations of life. If we follow his councils
and keep his commandments, he promises his protection and
blessing; but if we disregard and trample his commandments under foot, he has pronounced a curse upon such,
which he will execute in judgment. He has said them that
honor him, he will honor, and they that despise him shall
be lightly esteemed. Righteousness exalteth a nation, but
sin is a reproach to any people. Then the person who acts
most in accordance with those requirements upon which the
welfare of individuals and of nations is suspended, is the
true patriot, and the best friend to his country. While those

who disregard these things, whatever their political profession or their claims to patriotism may be. They are acting the part of enemies. When people have started in a way that they know to be wrong, and, because they are engaged in it, say they must go through with it, right or wrong, and hope the Lord will aid them in it, they are presumptuous to the highest degree.

We need not go to other countries and other people to find sins and sinners enough to subject our country to calamity and trouble, but there is sin enough, both north and south, to subject the nation to fearful calamities. I called her attention to many kinds of wickedness that abounds in our country, not only among those who were openly and professedly sinners, but among many professors of religion whose actions contradicted their professions. We were giving occasion to the adversary to speak reproachfully, whose example encouraged and justified the wicked, and was a stumbling block in the way of sinners. They could neglect the house of God and his appointed means of grace, and spend the Sabbath in ways of their own chosing, for their own pleasure and amusement, visiting and attending singings, &c.

Here she was touched at a tender point, for she had taught music on the Sabbath, and that, too, when there were appointments at the same time in the same neighborhood for preaching. She took it upon herself to justify the practice, and said she thought singing was as nice as preaching; that music was a part of worship, and she believed it was as right to sing as it was to preach; it had been impressed upon her mind from a child, that she ought to teach music, and she believed it was her duty, and she thought if she ever enjoyed religion in her life, it was when she was on the floor leading in music; and she had experienced as high feelings from good music, as ever she did under preaching.

I admitted that good music was very beautiful and very animating to the feelings; that it might and ought to be a part of religious worship; that it was a duty to practice it in that way: that it was a good and profiable exercise when attended to according to the scripture rule, "Sing with the spirit and with the understand." Said I, as it is an important part of worship, if we had not the opportunity of learning it on week days, so as to be able to perform it, there might be some propriety in teaching it on the Sabbath.

—8

But it is like many other things which are good and profitable in their proper places, but when used in tha place of something else, become very bad and injurious things. Whatever is positively commanded in the scriptures, we are safe and justifiable in practicing; but to put other things in the place of these, is a dangerous course and should be watched and guarded against. We have good authority for preaching on the Sabbath day, but none for teaching music on that day. And there is reason to believe that most of the performance of those singers is done without understanding, or caring much about the sentiment contained in the words connected with the music, and they do not attend to it as intelligent worship and service rendered to God, but as an exercise for animation and pleasure, which is a desecration of the Sabbath, Isaiah, LVIII, 13.

Many experience feelings of excitement, animation and pleasure from the drum and fife, as martial music, but it affords no edification or improvement in morality or religion. As to trusting to impressions, good and high feelings to teach us our duty and what is right, this is an unsafe course to pursue, and unless our *feelings* and impressions correspond with Bible precepts, it matters not how strong and animating they may be, they are wrong, delusive and dangerous. If strong impressions of a thing would prove it to be right and true, then the greatest heresies, absurdities and abominable idolatries that were ever held to or practiced by, or that ever disgraced human beings, might be proven to be right, for there is good reason to believe that they are the subjects of strong impressions and high feelings in their devotions.

She said she did not think they had such feelings as she had. I replied that whether they had or not, they would undergo more privation and self denial on account of their religion, and make greater sacrifices than professors of the christian religion of our time would do for theirs. And, said I, the disposition and actions of a great many who have a name in the church in the present day give good reasons to fear that they are as great strangers to a work of grace in their hearts as those deluded heretics and pagans. They have had some serious impressions, some elevated or lively feelings, but instead of obeying the gospel, believing in Christ, trusting and confiding in him alone for salvation, and thereby obtaining pardon and renovation, a new and clean heart and a right spirit, loving righteousness and hating iniquity, they have depended upon their impressions and feelings, and when these have subsided they have as good an appetite for sinful pleasures as ever they had, and as little a relish for holiness and the laws of God, and consequently live in habitual neglect of them.

By this time she was disposed to waive the subject, and to talk about farms, crops, etc., but I pursued the same subject till we came to the next house, where she made an excuse to stop, and I went on my way, thinking occasionally of what might possibly befall me for using so much freedom upon so delicate a subject guarded with so much vigilance and patriotic zeal.

Perhaps while on this tour, on calling at the house of one of my old neighbors, near to my next appointment, the old lady came out appearing surprised at my being there, and said she thought I would be afraid to come, for the report was out that I had been taken up. I smiled at hearing some things related by her. Said she, "You laugh." Said I, "It is as well to laugh as to look sad." She appeared alarmed, and said she would be afraid. Said I, "We are told not to fear them who kill the body but can do no more." She said the cavalry had been in that country hunting for and taking up Union men. Some had kept out of their way, and the cavalry said they would be back on Sabbath, and she thought people would be afraid to come out. Said I, "If they said they would be back at this time you need not be afraid; it will be more likely to be at some other time. Few ventured out and none were molested.

Not far from this time an appointment was made by the President of the Southern Confederacy, for a certain day to be observed as a day of fasting, humiliation and prayer. I heard that an appointment was made by a Baptist minister for a meeting of the people on that day at the church where he was pastor, but did not expect to be there himself. I felt a disposition to meet with them, not because I felt in duty bound to obey Davis, as the rightful ruler of the people, but I thought if people would attend to such a call in a proper manner, it would be profitable. But, contrary to calculation, the pastor was there, and after some time took his position before the pulpit, and remarked that he felt he had no more right to occupy the time that day than any other person, and he wished every one who desired it to take a part in the exercises of the day, and he wished none to go away with feelings mortified because they had not the opportunity of acting the part they felt it their duty to do.

After some other remarks had been make, and several persons at his request had made a prayer, he asked me if I wanted to come forward and occupy the time for a while. I was taken by surprise, not being aware that he knew me, for I had been at his appointments and he had taken no notice of me. I was also aware that the Baptist churches in that country had passed a rule against inviting ministers of other denominations into their pulpits, and I felt a little reluctant in going forward in the face of these considerations, but was fearful if I stayed back I might have occasion to regret it afterward; so I went forward and addressed the people about to the following effect : "It is not my wish to consume time with many remarks in reference to the occasion upon which we have met, for as we are all imperfect, fallible beings; whatever may be said on the subject by man there is a liability to error and mistake. But God has given us a rule to go by on such occasions as this is claimed to be. He has told us what is and what is not an acceptable fast to the Lord, and if we keep such a fast as he has required, we have his promise of a blessing. I acknowledge it may look like assuming much and I feel a delicacy in occupying time by reading what every man has in his own house and ought to be acquainted with : yet it is a fact that there are things in the Bible which some have never read nor even known that they are there, and much has been read and forgotten. And as we are prone to forget and lose sight of many important things contained in the scriptures, I have need to be reminded of them again and again, therefore, for our instruction and guide on the present occasion, we will attend to reading the LVIIIth chapter of Isaiah. After reading this chapter, which I would recommend my readers to turn to and read over carefully before proceding any farther, I remarked, if we would follow these instructions, and not be as the two brethren, who came desiring the Lord to do for them whatever they would ask, and requested for themselves that they might sit the one on his right and the other on his left hand in his kingdom, but after the example of our Savior in the garden, when he prayed, saying, "If it be possible let this cup pass from me, nevertheless, not my will but thine be done. And after the example of the Ninevites, who repented at the preaching of Jonah, when he said: "Yet forty days and Ninevah shall be destroyed." And the decree of the king and his nobles was, that every one should turn from his evil way and from the violence that is in his hands." And in so doing they obtained mercy and deliverence from the impending destruction.

Would we thus submit ourselves to the Lord, yielding hearty obedience to his requirements, we would have the faithful promise of the Almighty pledged for his favor and blessing. But if we pursue a different course, God will not be mocked, but we shall reap what we have sown, and bring upon ourselves that of which Jacob was afraid—a curse instead of a blessing. Gen. XXVII, 12.

Having closed by prayer and left the place to others, one who sometimes occupied the place of minister in the Baptist society, stepped forward trembling apparently under a high degree of nervous excitement, and said he could not, nor never expected to be able to express himself like some people, but he had something in his hand that he thought was very suitable to be read on that occasion ; and when he had read it what was it? What was the thing so very suitable for a season set apart for confession of sin, humiliation and prayer? It was one of those fierce and acrimonious publications, abounding with accusations and charges against northern people, of waging an unjust, cruel and wicked war against them, and advancing upon them for the purpose of bloodshed and murder, and destruction of life and property by fire and sword.

Some were astonished that in the face of what had been read from the Bible, any one could venture to introduce anything corresponding so exactly with the prophet's description of the manner in which the apostate Jews acted in his day: "For strife and debate and to smite with the fist of wickedness." Numbers, previous to this had made a mock of Bible reading and prayer as a means of avoiding the calamity of war, and said their guns were more to be depended upon then.

A short time previous to my departure from home, a sick soldier was brought to my house, where we nursed him for some time. While there his parents came to see him. His father, who was a Methodist minister and a secesh, knowing that I was not in favor of the seceding policy of the south, brought the charge against me in my own house, that I was

*—8

not disposed to go according to the apostolic rule : "To be subject to the powers that be." Although Union men were now in a great measure gagged, and had to be very modest and reserved, yet my feeling of independence and sense of personal rights were too strong to allow me tamely and silently to submit to such insinuations, under such circumstances. I asked how far the apostle himself followed the rule according to the construction he was putting upon it, and how far did he by his example justify such an interpretation of it? for if he had been subject to the requisitions of all the corrupt and idolatrious practices which the powers that existed where he was required to be conformed to, he would not have suffered persecution or martyrdom.

When the apostle said to the church of Rome, Romans XIII, 1, "Let every soul be subject to the higher powers, for there is no power but that of God; the powers that be are ordained of God, and whosoever resisteth the powers resisteth the ordinance of God, and they that resist shall receive to themselves damnation," he surely did not enjoin it upon them to submit and conform to those laws and requirements of the ruling powers and authorities which came in contact with, and were a violation of the laws of God; nor recognized that as being of God which was a violation of his laws; but only such as was in accordance with it; nor never taught them to obey man rather than God.

The correctness of this position was not denied. I then said, that it had been the boast of all the parties, north and south, that we had the best government in the world; that it was based upon the scriptures; that our laws were founded upon and authorized by Divine precepts; that God had acknowledged and sanctioned this claim, by many tokens of his approbation, and bright manifestations of his favor, in the unparalleled prosperity that had attended us as a nation. Said I, "This has been acknowledged on all hands, and the conclusion must necessarily follow that our government was one of the powers that was ordained of God, to which we are required to be subject. Why, then, were you not subject to it? and where did you get your authority for doing otherwise?"

This stopped the mouth of the accuser of our brethren, and the subject was dropped. I understood he scolded about it afterward, and claimed the right of secession through the sovereignty of the state, though he claimed to be under a democratic government, acording to which the majority must rule; yet I understood a large majority of the state in which he lived had voted to remain in the Union. And while a great outcry was making against coercing states, and compelling them to stay in the Union contrary to their wish, a minority had forced the state out.

At this time, I think, the federal army had got possession of the railroad from Memphis, Tenn., to Decatur, Ala., and it was reported that they would soon be at Columbus, Miss., and guards were placed along the public roads. Cavalry were stationed near Columbus, and a citizen of the country could not get to town without a pass; and when there, if they had not, they had to take the oath of allegiance to the Southern Confederacy, (to support Davis and his successors in office,) before they could get away. This I could not feel myself justifiable in doing, for I honestly believed there was no justifiable cause for seceding, and that it had been carried into effect by dishonest, unfair and wicked measures; consequently I kept myself where I would not be compelled to do what I believed to be wrong. It was a common saying that the required oath was not binding, because it was taken not of choice but by compulsion; and as their homes and all their treasures were there, they would take the oath but would not feel themselves bound to comply with it farther than suited their interests.

My reply to this mode of reasoning was, that if they did not consider their oath binding, those who administered it would, and if they were found acting contrary to it, they would be dealt with as if it was; and, for my part, I would ra'her suffer for not taking, than for breaking an unrighteous oath.

The Union people were hopeful that the rebellion would soon cease, and it was a common belief that the south was whipped, and that they had better give it up than to go on with it only to make matters worse. But some would not allow such a notion to be openly expressed, saying it had a tendency to discourage and weaken the cause.

Most of the soldiers who came to my house, who expressed their feelings on the subject, were anxious for the war to cease, upon almost any terms, and appeared to have very little hope of success in their cause, though there were some exceptions. Such was the dissatisfaction in the army it was thought they could not be kept together much longer, and many were deserting. They had to live on small rations, and there was fearful mortality in the camp. The prospect for provisions was uncommonly bad; so far as I was acquainted the wheat and oat crops were generally a failure, and there was the poorest prospect for corn there had been to the best of my recollection for forty years. It was thought by some that they would be compelled by famine to give up the war. And from the knowledge I had of the state of the supplies, I thought if the war continued, many women and children would have to suffer. Early corn had made all it could, and the drought, which had been very severe, still continued. Some were out of old grain, and many scarce or without salt and some were concealing it; and it was said that in some places people were making salt from the drainings of their smoke house floors.

CHAPTER V.

CIRCUMSTANCES OF ESCAPE FROM THE SOUTH.

It was a short time previous to my leaving home, I returned to its owner a mule, which had been worked on my farm. On my way, as was required of me, from some source, I do not remember what, I gave notice to some of the citizens of the country through which I passed, that they were required to go to Columbus and take the oath of allegiance. While stopping with a man on this business he told me of the death of an acquaintance who was to be burried that day. The son of the deceased, having been influenced by his father to go into the army, had been brought home sick, had died, and been buried a day or two before.

The man with whom I was conversing, speaking of the deceased to be buried that day, said: "He and his wife came to my house just one year ago to-day, and were in high spirits in view of the seceding of the South, and said that in twelve months our country would be in the most happy and prosperous condition that it ever had been."

After returning the mule to its owner, and traveling several miles across a section of country where was scarcely a man to be seen, nearly all being women and children, and of the former many were widows, I arrived at the house of a doctor who had known me from his childhood, and from him I obtained a certificate to the following effect: That my constitution and state of health were not sufficient to undergo the exposure and perform the duties of a soldier.

Another doctor, who had been acquainted with me from my boyhood, certified the same. I went before a magistrate and was sworn to the correctness of the above.

On the following day, which was Saturday, there was an appointment for a meeting to muster and enroll the names of all the men residing in the district to which I belonged, between the ages of thirty-five and fifty. From eighteen to thirty-five had been conscripted, and their time had about expired, after which, conscripts who had neither volunteered nor reported themselves were to be looked after, and some had been keeping themselves concealed for some time in the woods, and on that night (Friday preceding the muster) according to previous appointment, a company of twelve were going to start for the Federal government. A part of them were to start from my brother's house. Among the twelve I had a son and six nephews. After or before my return home that evening, two cavalrymen come to my house and wished to know if there was any outhouse that they could lodge in that night. I told them that they could lodge in the house with us if they would. They appeared backward about doing it, and kept their horses tied up during the night. After dark I told them I had to be absent for awhile on business.

I then went to my brothers to see the last of those who were about leaving. My son was not there, but I witnessed the parting scene with those that were, some of whom we can meet no more in time. I then returned home, not knowing but that those soldiers would take me into close quarters in the morning, but when they arose in the morning some of the family heard one of them say to the other, "No Yankees have passed the road last night." The truth was, they had been sent to guard the road, which was near a quarter of a mile from the house.

That morning I went to the captain's house, saw his commission and what he was authorized to do, and gave him my certificate. He said it was all sufficient, so far as he was concerned, and ought to satisfy any person, but if I should be drafted, he supposed it would not be of any benefit to me, as there would be a military surgeon appointed who had the examination of the drafted, who would have to abide by his decision.

After this I had other business to attend to, which detained me till afternoon. On returning home my family informed me that I and all others in the neighborhood who had not taken the oath of allegiance, were required to go to Columbus and take the oath on the next Monday, and if we did not, we would be taken by an armed force. The person by whom this notice was sent, having asked what they would do with a person, if after they had taken him, he would not take the oath, he was told that they would confiscate his property, and send him to Lincolndom. I was now brought into a straight to know what to do, and had but a short time to decide the case in. To leave my family was intolerable to think of; and to do that which I believed to be a great sin against God and the interests of my country, was too much to submit to. I thought it possible my family were a little mistaken in regard to the true state of the case, and I would go and see a neighbor who had been to town and knew what the fact of the case was. But I was so well satisfied that they were right that I fed my horse and left it to eat and rest till I would return. I told my family to get such things ready for my journey as they could, that were necessary, for I expected to leave that night. So I went on foot to the neighbor's house, and learned that the information was indeed correct, and inquired particularly with regard to the form and substance of the required oath, for he had taken it, and I had learned that some who had taken it had said it was as long as the moral law. I learned that it not only bound a person to support the constitution and laws of the Southern Confederacy, but to be subject to and support J. Davis and his successors in office. This was more than I could be reconciled to, but I was rather censured and did not seem to receive much sympathy.

From there I went to my brother's where I had been the night before. I wished to have some conversation with him before I would leave. When I arrived another person was there who remained for some time, and I waited for him to leave before I would introduce the trying subject; and when left to ourselves found we had much the same views of what was the best and safest course to pursue. And after a short interview with, and taking leave of a bereft family, I returned to my own to join with them in making preparations for my departure as best I could. It was a trying season. My name was on the list of those liable to draft, which was expected the next week. On Monday I was required to take an oath, which if I failed to do I had no doubt but I would be one of the drafted number, and then would be in a safe box, for though I had a good excuse for exemption, yet, as I knew of others being pressed into the service, who were legally exempt from and actually unfit for military service, I therefore had nothing to hope for in that line.

But how could I bear to be separated from my family, and leave them to take the chances that might follow? I said if I knew they would send us in safety to the Union lines, if they took everything from us, I was heartily willing to stay and see them out with it. But it was thought if they started with me I never would get there, and while I was out of their hands I had better keep out. But as the trial was a hard one to submit to, some of the family asked why I could not do like some others and stay at home. Feelings of abhorence seemed to arise at the thought, and I replied something after this manner : "The Confederacy is a wicked and unjustifiable undertaking, and they are making use of wicked and unjustifiable measures to accomplish their object, I am not going to take an oath to assist them."

Night came on before our preparations were through with, and notwithstanding the exciting circumstances of the occasion, I felt disposed to occupy a part of our last hours together to reading the scriptures and prayer to the God of our fathers, and thought it very remarkable that I was enabled to go through with the whole exercise with so much composure and submission, and so heartily commit us with all the unknown events of the future, to the disposal of an all wise and good Sovereign.

A list of the names and ages of the family was furnished to take with me—but I leave the particular details of the parting scene to be read in verses composed upon that subject.

Between the hours of eight and nine o'clock that night, the 12th of July, 1862, we parted with the deliberate calculatinn that one whole family, which had been together a few nights before, would never all meet together in time. The next week I would have left home, if permitted, to attend my appointments in Alabama, and had been intending to go to a factory on Bear creek in some of my tours, as I had to go the greater part of the distance there to fill my appointments I said to my family it might be before I would get clear away, I might find that they were not going to execute their threats, and that I would be back after filling my appointments as before, and if people inquired for me they could tell them they did not look for me back till after the time of those appointments.

Thus I departed from my country and kindred, not knowing whither I went. I had been sick and was then able to do a half day's work if I would rest the remainder of the day. I could not stand it to do much riding in the sun, but the circumstances under which I was placed gave me a favorable opportunity to effect my escape before I was suspected of having such designs.

Two of my nephews, who had sometime before started out on foot to attend some appointments, were so strongly suspected of having started to the Yankees, that some men would hardly be persuaded not to follow and bring them back; but now they were gone indeed, and their appointments filled as best they might. I also arose, took the horse to pass those suspicious regions by night, and escape from what might be called *Sodom in Egypt, and to flee to Abraham's bosom, there to remain till I should receive word and hear that they who sought to destroy the Union are dead.

Thus I set out, traveling sometimes along the road and sometimes through woods and along by-paths, as caution and prudence might dictate to be best. As it was about full moon, I could see to travel through the woods and along private ways, so as to shun danger. In this way I traveled with a heavy heart during the night, and until an hour or two by sun on Sabbath morning; and though I felt deeply concerned for my Union neighbors and brethren whom I had left, yet I felt a degree of assurance that the church would in some way be shielded and protected by Providence—so confident of it was I at times, that I almost resolved to risk my fortune with them. But I knew that though David had the promise of a kingdom, he had to fly from Saul and Absolem to save his life, and our Savior had to be taken into Egypt to prevent Herod from destroying him, so I thought it probably was necessary for me to go away to secure life and to accomplish some wise and good design of Providence, for I had no doubt but the Lord would by this war accomplish some great and lasting good for the best interests of His cause and kingdom in the world, notwithstanding the great wickedness of men in getting up and carrying on the war with all its dreadful calamities. I thought, as I said when leaving my family, that it might be that we who were leaving our families, might be as Joseph, sent to prepare for the preservation of others.

When I arrived on Sabbath morning where I expected to

---

*Southern Confederacy.

spend the day, the man of the house was still in bed, having got home late in the night after visiting and taking provisions to his friends and relatives, who had been in a half starved condition in the southern army, then stationed, I think, at Tupulo, between Corinth and Pontotock. He was a Union man, but had a son or two in the rebel army. I asked to have a bed as soon as would be convenient, as I was weary and feeble, and needing sleep and rest.

There was preaching in the neighborhood that day, and my host invited me to go to it, and perhaps thought it strange that I did not. I told him I was in feeble health, tired and could not well stand the heat of the sun, and could not, in justice to myself, and without risk of damage, go with him.

When I retired it was with difficulty that I could get any relief from distress; for from fatigue, loss of sleep and trouble of mind, when I would get into a doze, I would be roused up in a smothering and almost dying condition' and, whether asleep or awake, my family was on my mind, and the strong desires of my heart were almost constantly going forth in their behalf to the hill whence salvation cometh. After some time my sleep became more composed and refreshing, so that by evening I was considerably revived, and could have some satisfaction in conversation. Their preacher came with them from church, and though a great secesh, we had an evening of pleasant conversation. I retired early to bed, telling them not to think strange if I was not there in the morning. They supposed I would not leave till after breakfast. I said as the weather was very hot I could not stand the sun very well, I expected to travel by moonshine while it was cool. Being asked if I would be at my appointment the last of the week. I said if nothing took place to prevent it, I would be there.

After midnight, I set out again, and, after traveling about ten miles, took my breakfast with one of my old neighbors, and after passing what had been my home in Alabama, I stopped and dined with another neighbor, where I tried to sleep, but failed. I inquired for some one who would be going to the factory, intending if I could, to get in company with some of my acquaintances in the country who were going there, I would go with them, as I had some southern money that whold soon be worthless to me. I thought I would give it for thread and get some of the people there to take it to my house, when passing to Columbus. This would be serviceable to them, and give a chance to hear from me; but I could hear of no such chance, and as the cavalry were running around, I did not wish to go without some one who had been acquainted with me.

As the day was getting cloudy, I went a few miles farther to a shop, to get shoes put on my horse. While there waiting for this to be done, I had the information from an acquaintance there present, that the cavalry were frequently passing between there and the factory, and if they came on me and I had no pass, I would stand a chance of being set on foot. They had, a short time before, taken the last bushel of corn a widow had, which she had lately bought. He invited me to spend the night with him, but I thought best not to do so, but went a little distance back, took across toward another road, which I concluded to travel. On the way I called on a man for instruction concerning the roads, whom I knew to be a Union man, and who had been hunted by the cavalry. While there, another man living near one of my places of preaching, called and urged me strongly to go and spend the night with him, and when I would not agree to it, he asked me if I would be at my appointment on Sabbath. I said, if nothing prevented I would.

While thus detained on my way across, a company of cavalry passed and I fell into the road behind them, and traveled all night, except a little while that I sat beside a tree near the road, and perhaps slept a little while my horse rested.

Having passed Pikeville and crossed several water courses, at daybreak I came in sight of a house by the roadside, where I thought I saw a cavalry horse standing. I left the road, and tying my horse in a secure place, returned cautiously to learn the truth of the matter, but finding nothing I remounted and rode up to the house, where I saw plenty of tracks. A youth who had just crept out of bed came to the road. I asked if there were any Yankees about there? He said, No, but the southern cavalry had just gone up the road. I asked the distance to the factory and asked many questions concerning the citizens between that road and the road leading to the factory. After following the road a short distance, I took a private way in the opposite direction, which led to a house where I tried to get my horse fed, but could not. I was directed to Squire Stidem's, who was brother to the one I had heard speak the summer before on Sugar

creek, and thought him the only honest man out of six that
spoke that day, so I thought I was getting to the right
place. There I got breakfast and my horse fed and took
a bed in a house to myself, expecting there to sleep and rest
till morning. But before I had enjoyed my slumbers long
toe people began to sing in a house near by, and their music
being much like what I was used to at home, roused me
from sleep and so excited my feelings that I no longer felt
like sleep; so I left the dormitory and shared in the music.

The Squire had an uneasy and disquieted appearance, as
if in great anxiety and suspense of mind, which was more
or less characteristic of all present. He said the way things
were there he had no heart to work, and that was the way he
was putting in his time.

The pieces sung, being the same that I had been used to
at home, and the voices resembling some in my own family,
they strongly reminded me of those I had left, which
wrought deeply on my feelings. It was an exciting occasion
for several reasons. The Squire and his wife, I think were
of different religious persuasions—Baptist and Methodist.
The war was the all absorbing subject. and I think the
question was up whether the war was or was not providen-
tial; whether the Almighty did or did not design to accomplish something by it. As I was tolerably familiar with the
scriptures, they detained me for a time finding prophesies
and texts of scripture and giving my views of some of them,
and in giving a list of portions of scripture for their consideration. Being charged with running away, I humored it
as a joke and let it pass.

Some time previous some dozen or more men had been taken from that region by cavalry, and had been confined in
the Columbus prison in Mississippi. It is said that all except one had been released and on their return had passed
the day before. It had been reported that the one detained
was to be shot. His wife started to Columbus to see him,
but said that some distance from town the road was guarded
by soldiers, who would not let her pass, and she had returned
without seeing him. She and her child came to the Squire's
that day, and were exciting objects of pity and commisera-
tion. I was informed that the cause of those men being taken up, was that in another county a company of men had
organized, calling themselves the Regulators, who were going around among the citizens, and if they did not talk and

do according to their liking they dealt with and regulated them and their property according to their own notion. In view of this state of things, the men in the locality where those were arrested, had organized into a *home protection body*, for the purpose of preventing any person or his property from being molested contrary to law. The Regulators hearing of this, went and reported that they were preparing to resist the Confederacy; and, upon this, the cavalry were sent to arrest them.

Several people were coming in, some of whom knew me and had heard me preach while residing in that state. I began to feel that it was too public a place for me. I also learned that scouts from the confederate army south of Corinth sometimes passed that way; so I paid the Squire a dollar in southern currency and again took through the woods, along paths converging to the direction of the highway, and when I came to it, it was all cut up with fresh tracks— I supposed of cavalry horses, going in the direction I was traveling. As I thought some of them might be coming back my policy was to keep a sharp lookout far ahead, so as to see them first; and as the road was on a dividing ridge, with deep hollows on each side, hoped to be able to dash suddenly down and conceal myself among the hills before they would see or get near to me.

It was not long before I saw at a distance something resembling that of which I was afraid of, and—for I was feeling quite wild—I was soon out of sight of the road, behind a hillside abounding with grass, weeds, briars and vines, and I pursued my course along a deep hollow, corresponding with the course of the road, till I could venture to ascend to the road again; soon after which a dark and stormy looking cloud came up behind me, and I thought it might prevent any that were behind from coming on, and might serve as a wall between us. The cloud being driven by a strong wind, I soon had to get into a house or take the storm. I had the fortune to be received into a house where the woman was alone. From her I learned the distance and rout to Russelville, and that a company of cavalry had gone along that road a while before. I learned that she was acquainted at Russelville, and asked her many questions with regard to churches, religious denominations, &c. She supposed I was a minister and wished to know my faith, and though of a different belief, she professed much respect for people of my persuasion, for she had been raised or educated by them. The time was passed in interesting conversation till the storm was over. Then afterward, while at a house where I was waiting for the horse to lay in a supply for a good night's travel, a man came along who said that the cavalry were going to camp within a mile of there. I asked if there was any way to go to Russelville without going among them. I was told there was none but where a person would be liable to met with the pickets. I said if there was, I would prefer going around, as I had been told that they did not always treat people civilly. They said as I was a traveler they would not be apt to mistreat me, and thought my chances would be better to go right through than for the pickets to find me trying to get round; so I set off, determined to make the venture.

As I went I thought it might be that my course was not a justifiable one, and that I was going to be taken back; and if so, I would submit to my lot, be it what it might. So I committed my case into the hands of the Wise Disposer of all events, and pushed forward toward the dread place, where I could hear frequent discharges of fire arms.

Before getting to the place I had devised a way to deceive them, by telling them nothing but the truth, if they required me to give an account of myself, which I think would have had the desired effect, and I would have felt myself justifiable in being a deceiver.

When I came in sight they all appeared to be busily engaged, some making fires and some attending to their horses, and some to their arms, and a company was standing across the road shooting off their pistols—I supposed because they had been exposed to the storm. When I came to them some had their pistols up as if about to shoot. I addressed them, calling them gentlemen, and asked them if they were going to shoot. My young beast, showing signs of being afraid, passed hastily by them. I permitted it to go without much restraint and passed them without being halted or asked a single question.

How strangely and agreeably disappointed I felt! I felt as if it was the Lord's doing, and that it was a marvelous deliverence, and there was a great reviving and uprising of spirits within me, and I went on my way feeling quite relieved and light.

This was after sunset and near the bridge on Big Bear

creek, over which I soon passed, and meeting a small squad of soldiers, they asked if I had seen the cavalry. Said I "they are camping a short distance back." All was right, and onward we all went. I felt a strong determination to make that the last night I would be found inside the rebel lines. How strange that I had got by them so easily! Owing to my clothing they perhaps took me for a citizen of that country, and if so were well deceived, for I was nearly a hundred miles from home. My coat and saddlebags being under my cloak, perhaps they were not seen.

In my travel that night I passed up and down some tremendous hills, and through deep and dark ravines, while the stars shone, passed towering banks and roots of trees far above. The way was so dark and doubtful below it made the descent very slow; after which was what, by moonshine appeared to be an extensive and beautiful plain, where, traveling till weary and drowsy, I left the road a little way, and took my seat at the root of a spreading topped tree—

> Awhile to enjoy a transient repose,
> In a strange world of wilderness and woes.

But fearing that some straggler might chance to leave me afoot, I loosed thence and went forward again, till it appeared as if I had gone far enough to be at Russelville, and having passed a house some distance, and fearing lest by some means I had lost the right way, I turned and went back to the house to inquire, but found a house without inhabitants and went on again, resolved to take the first private way I could find, supposing I would not have to go far without finding some residence. After a while I found and followed the desired way, which soon began to descend, and down, onward down, it did still descend, till I wondered much where the thing would end—

> When lo, a great valley, all in field,
> And corn was the fruit I saw it did yield.

There was a gate through which I had to pass to keep in the road, which, a half mile farther through a corn field, stopped at a house. There I had my horse fed, and, as the chickens were crowing, laid me down in the porch and slept till the dawn of day, when I was conducted through fields across to the road leading to Russellville, where I intended to stop and write a letter to my people, but on arriving there a cloud was on the countenances of the people, visibly indicative of something unpleasant. The doors were shut next the streets, along which scarcely any were passing. All appeared quiet and still, and all the men I recollect of seeing, except one at the closed door of a drug store, were in back porches from the street, and when I would call at a house a woman would first appear, and a man cautiously afterwards, and after passing I could see numbers of men in back porches.

I then learned that the mail had been stopped the day before, so my intended home communication was cut off. I asked at a drug store for eyewater, but was told they had none, and was directed to a doctor's shop some distance beyond town. I thought they looked at me very suspiciously, and I had gone but a little distance when I met two little boys in the street. Said one: Are you not afraid the Yankees will catch you? Said I, are there any Yankees about here? He said there were two thousand of them about a half a mile from there. I then, in part, understood the signs of the times; and this was no bad news to me. I was inclined to go to their camp, but as it was a little out of the way to Tuscumbia, I concluded not to go.

The doctor to whom I had been directed being absent, I went forward, and passed a place that had been occupied by soldiers, where dogs were devouring the remains of horses that lay in and about the road. After passing a short distance from there, I came opposite a house near the road, and saw a man passing through the yard whose countenance I thought I could read.

By this time the sun was quite warm, and I was tired and thirsty, and asked if I could get some water and rest with them awhile, and being made welcome to do so, was soon satisfied that I was right in my opinion of the man.

From him I learned that there had been a little battle, in which some horses were killed, where I saw those remains, and perhaps two or three Union soldiers had been wounded there, and for a time had been in the hands of the Russellville doctors. He also informed me that a company of Yankee soldiers had been at Russellville the day before, and had taken, I think, some of the citizens and all of the doctors, but one, to Tuscumbia without telling the reason for so doing. As cotton had been burned at some places through the country, and there was also a report that a wounded Union officer had been mistreated by the physicians, it was conjectured that on account of one or both of these charges those men had been arrested, and that would account for the state of things I had seen in town, though this man thought the boys were mistaken, and that it was a confederate regiment that had stationed themselves in the fork of the road, for he knew that they had designed to occupy that position to cut off the Yankees when they went to Russellville. He had seen one of their scouts crossing through the glade a short time before.

I was glad I had not gone to them, but after a little reflection upon what I had seen, said I thought the boys were right. He asked if I had noticed the tracks of the horses; he said if he had seen them he could easily tell which it was. When I had described them he said it was the Northern soldiers, and they had disappointed the others.

After resting and learning what I could with regard to the roads, the distance to the Union pickets, to Tuscumbia, Florence, &c., I set out again, and as I was getting to the picket I met those men who had been taken from Russellville, and now on their return from Tuscumbia. I was halted by the guards and asked where I was going. At first they refused to let me pass, saying that they had received orders to let no mere people pass. I conjectured from that that they felt themselves in a dangerous situation, and I of course felt the more anxious to get beyond those uncertain and dangerous localities.

After some conversation I was sent forward to an officer posted farther on my way, and from him to another higher officer, who asked me if I was willing to take the oath of allegiance to the government. I told him that I had no objections to taking it, as it had formerly been administered. He asked if I had a family; their condition, circumstances under which I had left them, reasons for leaving, &c. This brought the scenes and circumstances of those tender relationships so vividly to view that my manliness failed, and my usual strength of nerve and power of self command gave way, so that I had to ask him to bear with me till I could properly state the facts of the case. He showed some disposition for indulgence and sympathy in the case, and spoke of himself having the trial of leaving his friends

I was afterward conducted by a guard past several other

companies, posted at different places along the road, and had many questions to answer and to hear many a profane expression. My conductor was so exceedingly profane that I gave him a serious reproof and admonition. But it seemed to me afterwards that he used profane language without being conscious of doing so. I soon began to feel badly disappointed and deeply depressed in spirit on account of the great wickedness so visible among the soldiers. There was a striking similarity between my inward feelings and the strong exclamation of Jonah, chap. II, 3, 5 : All thy billows and thy waves passed over me; the waters compassed me about, even to the soul.

As I was getting to an officer's tent in camp, many came around full of curiosity, but not all in conformity to the rules of civility. The officer occasionally ordered them away. He asked me where I was from. Being told the state and county of which I was a resident, he asked if I was acquainted in Columbus; if I knew several merchants of that place whom he named, and if I was acquainted with several business houses and important places in and about Columbus, which he mentioned. When all these questions were answered apparently to his satisfaction, he asked a number of questions with regard to the state of things in that country.

After I had answered his questions honestly to the best of my ability, I said to him that one of the greatest objections I had to the country I had left, I was sorry to say it, I had found to prevail among them there. He asked what that was. I said it was profane swearing. He made rather light of it and said that soldiers must swear some. Said he : "The soldiers swore in Washington's time." I admitted they did, but not with his approbation, but it was a source of mortification to him, and he used his influence and authority to put it down. I said it was no light matter, for just so sure as it was true that those who took the name of God in vain should not be held guiltless, so sure it was that unless they change their course they would suffer for it, and disappointment and calamity awaited them. I said I had been sadly disappointed and discouraged by what I had witnessed. I felt it to the soul.

After some questions and examinations with regard to what I had with me, he wrote something to be given to Gen. Thomas. He and Adjutant Flint were in the office. The paper being presented to them and its contents read, they did not add many more questions. But I was so deeply affected by what I had witnessed that I had to disclose some of my views and feelings to those in high places. Gen. Thomas appeared grave and consistent, but Flint appeared rather airy and flighty in his manners and conversation, and had a high notion of what their superior numbers and military skill could effect, and was confident of success and of a speedy termination of the war. I had occasion to tell him that according to the scriptures, the race was not to the swift nor the battle to the strong, and that no king is saved by the multitude of his host, and that a curse is pronounced upon those who trust to an arm of flesh.

I was required to give my age, residence and occupation, and to take the oath of allegiance, or the parole of honor. I chose the latter, from the consideration that I had not means to travel far, and might have to spend some time among people who were prejudiced against the Administration, and by having it to say that I had not taken the oath, I could have more influence with them for good. I labored perhaps for an hour for some additional conditions to be expressed in the parole before I would sign it, but could not prevail. Flint had the business to attend to, and in his conversation told me that he had been brought up strictly by religious parents. As I was speaking of the importance of being prepared for the worst, under circumstances of so much danger and uncertainty of life, he remarked that he had lived an honest life, paid his just debts, injured no one, and now if he should fall while he was engaged in so good a cause, he thought that when the angel of mercy came to look over his case, his tear would blot out his few short comings. I said he was jesting and could not be sincere in his pretensions, for if he was acquainted with the doctrines of the Bible he must know better. He said he had been raised a good Presbyterian, and had been brought up to read the Bible. As he had used language in my presence not strictly moral, I asked if it was not a pity, if they had raised him a good Presbyterian, that he had not remained so. He claimed to be sincere in what he had said. I said if he had been educated according to the Presbyterian rules, such notions were utterly unworthy of his raising.

They gave me a pass with orders for free transportation over the river. When leaving, Flint gave me three dollars to assist me on my way. As I thanked him for his kindness he said he would take it out in prayers, and asked to be remembered in my daily devotions.

While detained at the General's office there was a great fall of rain, which helped to revive my hopes for a support being made at home for my forsaken family. That night I lodged at Murdock's, in South Florence. As a Union officer's wife from Illinois, was boarding there, the landlady kindly cautioned me, (as she understood I was from the south), against anything that might mortify the feelings of her boarder, who, she said, was a great Union woman.

That night and next morning being rainy, I had a time of refreshing slumber and rest. The lady from Illinois was talking of returning home, and it was thought the rain would raise the river so that boats could pass. My bill in the morning was two dollars.

Having crossed the river and passed through Florence. I pursued my course with considerable depression of spirits, under the impression that the war would not close as soon as I expected, but that the northern people had to meet with disasters and calamities as well as the south, for correction, humiliation and purification, before the war would end.

While my horse was feeding at noon I was employed, according to a long established rule, of reading a portion of scripture every day, in reading the XXIVth of Isaiah, which, in a regular course of reading occupied my time that day, and I was strongly impressed with the idea that it might have reference to what was then in operation, and that people who were trying to make their escape from evil in one place might be overtaken by it in another; so that he who fleeth from the noise of the fear shall fall into the pit. He that cometh up out of the midst of the pit shall be taken in the snare.

That evening I passed a cotton factory, I think on a stream called Shoal creek. Near the factory, by some houses on the way down the creek, the hurried movements of the people, tone of voice and expression of countenance, bespoke alarm, anxiety and distress. I soon learned that a child several years old was missing, supposed to be drowned by attempting to cross the creek on a foot way of plank while the water was rising, and perhaps moving some of the planks from their position. As I was crossing, many were searching the creek, which flowed rapidly. This had no tendency to diminish my depression of spirits, but somehow there was an increasing impression that evil awaited me in the course I was going, and things were more and more forbidding. The roads rocky and hilly, my horse too young to stand traveling well, no chance to sell it, short of money, crops just laid by and no call for hands to work, my prospects were anything but flattering. In Ohio I had relations and thought of going there, but lacked the means, and unless I was able to get into business a while was not able to go.

When I had got about to the Tennessee line, if I recollect rightly, I found an unsuspicious youth, from whom I learned a number of things with regard to the people and country there that I considered important for me to know. I inquired for some one who he suposed could give general information with regard to the state of things in that country, and the chance for employment. He directed me to a Mr. Canedy, where I remained over night, and got information concerning persons and places where there was a probability of finding employment. There I had the opportunity of examining an atlas, and saw, as I thought that Illinois was the state to which I should go, and resolved to go back to the river and take a boat.

The first thing was to get into business to get means to pay my way. So next morning I set out in quest of work; first to a mechanic's then to a brick yard. They had got a supply of hands. Then to a factory, but it was stopped for want of wool. I thought of going then to Tuscumbia, but learned that the creek was so high people did not like to cross. My informant said he was going the next day to Florence : by that time the creek would be down, and if I would be at his house early we would go together. I inquired for a good place to stop at, and if he knew of any clocks out of repair. He directed me to a Mr. Street, and thought he also had a clock out of repair. I found the old man ready to take me in, saying, "We are directed not to be unmindful to entertain strangers," but he had got his clock put in order.

As I could get no work to do and the day was not half gone, and I had seen a chance at the factory, I asked if they would like to have preaching that night. He thought it would be acceptable, and said we would see the man who had charge of the house ; so the appointment was made and filled accordingly.

The old man is what is called a Two Seed Baptist. I had not been long in his house when he began to present his peculiar doctrine. I received it kindly, though not pretending to have adopted it as my belief, but admitted that there were portions of scripture that appeared to favor his views, and joined in with him quoting and pointing out texts that might be construed in that way. Thus that subject was disposed of. Afterward we had much interesting conversation upon experimental religion, and he treated me more like an old acquaintance and particular friend than a stranger. He showed me his meadow and beautiful springs of water. He treated me as did Hezakiah the Messengers sent to him from the king of Babylon, after Hezakiah's recovery from sickness. He told me of his negroes sold, amount of money, &c., yet everything about him was of the plainest and commonest kind, and he appeared to be contented. Some were uneasy, lest they should loose their negroes, but he appeared to think if they would take his out of his way he would not grieve about it, for he had more satisfaction while making the money to buy them, than he had with them when he owned them.

Next morning when I left he would have no recompense, but repeated the apostle's words with regard to entertaining strangers, and requested me if ever in the country again to call on him.

Before reaching Florence I was informed that Morgan was committing depredations in the country through which I intended to pass, and where one or two days' travel would have taken me. I now thought I saw that things were working for the best for me. I learned when passing Shoal creek that the lost was not yet found.

Having retraced my steps to Tuscumbia, as I was approaching the General's office, one of the guards met me and said: "Your people are come." I had informed them of the company that had left my neighborhood before I did, and had given some of their names, and requested that if they came there they would let them know that I had passed north. They had arrived there the evening before, one week from the night they started from Dixey, and that night one week before had witnessed my departure from home. I was not long in finding them, and was not a little rejoiced to find that they had all got safely to that point, though poor, pitiful, bleached, weather-beaten looking objects; lean, pale and dirty, tired and sleepy, having made their way more than one hundred miles through field and woods, among hills and hollows, mountains and valleys, across creeks and swamps, through brambles and briars, exposed to rain, dew heat and thirst; sometimes short of provisions, exhausted and hungry, and sometimes pursued by men and dogs. But out of them all they had been delivered, and were waiting for conveyance to Columbus, Kentucky. So we rested together till Monday, supplied from the fulness of Uncle Sam's charity, and could with deep interest relate the memorable scenes and incidents of the past week, feeling the interposing hand of a special Providence had been very visible in effecting our escape and deliverance from the many dangers through which we had passed.

On Sabbath one of my nephews preached to a part of the soldiers, where, notwithstanding the serious attention of some, there were strong indications of infidelity in the army; and some of the officers professed to have more confidence in powder and ball, and to trust more to them for success than to the Lord. By conversing with the soldiers I found some of them as totally ignorant of the Bible doctrine of salvation as the most ignorant backwoods southerner that I had ever conversed with. Their morality and good works, which evidently were very imperfect, and the cause in which they were engaged, was the foundation of their hope of eternal life; and some were Universalists.

Some, when kindly admonished against some evils in camp, replied that their preachers participated with them in such things. All of which seemed to say that the north as well as the south were snared in a delusion, and were going to be subjected to sad reverses, disasters and disappointments in their calculations, and that there was yet a day before us the coming of which many of us would not abide.

> Who may abide the coming day,
> And then sustain no harm or loss?
> Fire and soap must cleanse away
> Pollution, filth and marring dross.
>
> When fire gold doth well refine,
> And soap the filth from cloth clean,
> The gold will then more brigetly shine,
> The cloth together close adhere.

When God has thus refined the land,
 And shall with peace or order bless,
An image from the artist's hand
 Shall then appear in righteousness.

Though greatly we have been at fault,
 In evil long we took delight ;
The Lord the righteous will exalt
 To bliss and honor in his sight.

The nation who the Lord obeys,
 Submitting to His wise command,
He will to wealth and honor raise,
 And long preserve them in the land.

But nations who forget the Lord,
 And will against his laws rebel,
He them will scourge with plague and sword,
 And downward turn them into hell.

CHAPTER VI.

OCCURRENCES ON THE WAY TO MOUNT ZION, ILLINOIS.

Monday morning I tried to make some disposition of my horse, so that I could go with the rest of the company, but failed to do it. I then thought I would go to Eastport, and take passage on a boat, intending to leave my horse with some person to keep as their own until I should call for it, as I still cherished the fond hope that it would not be long before I could again return in peace.

As I knew that the citizens of Marion county, Ala., had been trading with the northern people at Eastport, I thought I would write a letter to my people, and leave it at Eastport to be conveyed by some of the Alabamians, and mailed at Pikeville. This met the wishes of the company, and several of them loaned me a small sum of money to pay my expenses to Illinois. As some of my nephews had an uncle and some other relations in Macon county, near Decatur, in that state, they expected to go to that point.

I set out for Eastport, leaving them still waiting for the train. As I was passing some soldiers near the stream that flows from the Tuscumbia springs, I heard one of them say: "There goes that old *butternut*," which was the first time I recollect to have heard the appellation applied to a man, and did not comprehend its whole import, as it is now understood.

It was now late, and the distance I think is about thirty miles. The most of the way was along lanes through a rich valley, where the traveler has to go many miles among farms without passing a house, and when he comes in sight of a dwelling, it is like a little town, and if he is a Bible reader, is reminded of the language of the prophet, Isaiah V, 8, 9, "Woe unto them that join house to house, that lay fields to

*—10

fields till there is no place that may be placed alone in the midst of the earth." Of a truth many houses shall be desolate, even great and fair without inhabitant.

I failed to dispose of my horse, and stopped twelve miles short of Eastport, at a house where I lodged with a secessionist, who treated me kindly, without charge. On arriving at Eastport, I found that the trade with the Alabamians had been stopped, and my last hope of communication cut off. I failed, also, of getting on a boat, but was kindly treated by the soldiers. I then fell in with a man of Irish descent, who advised me not to sell my beast there, but to take it to St. Louis, where, after paying for transportation, I could get more for it than I could get there. He had bought a mule which he said he was going to take there to sell.

We learned that at Pittsburg Landing we could get on a boat; so we set off in haste, rode till after night, and stopped one mile short of the Landing. The day following we got all necessary arrangements made and took passage on the steamer Sunshine, with the promise of being landed at St. Louis on the third day, but the boat was pressed to convey government horses to Eastport, to and from which we were taken during the night, and did not start for St. Louis until the evening after. My comrade insisted that I should take cabin passage, but I told him that the present condition of myself and family would not justify me in doing so, and I would be at no expense that I could reasonably avoid.

The boat traveled slowly, and stopped several times to take on and put off loading, so that we were detained several days longer than we had contracted for. During this time I was greatly annoyed by the profanity and vices of the hands and passengers; but I got in favor with the carpenter, who gave me leave to keep my clothes and provisions in his shop, and occupy it myself when he was not using it. He gave me the key so that I could go in and out at pleasure. There I could retire and read for hours without annoyance, and there I lodged at night, and also enjoyed some seasons of pleasant conversation with the carpenter. He was of an opinion, like the Jews with regard to circumcision: that unless a man be baptised he cannot be saved, and I supposed by baptism he meant immersion. He said if I could disprove the correctness of that belief from the Bible, he would like me to do it. I told him I had no pleasure in controversy, and I would have him to understand that in all the only object I had in view was that he might be profited by it. I said if he was candid, I thought I could prove so plainly from the Bible that a person could be saved without water baptism, that he would acknowledge it himself. I asked him if he thought the word Paradise, where it was used in the New Testament, meant Heaven, or a state of happiness. He said he did. Said I, "You remember that when the Savior was crucified between two thieves, that when one of them reviled, the other prayed to him, saying: 'Lord remember me when thou comest into thy kingdom,' the Lord said : 'To-day thou shalt be with me in Paradise.' There he had to hang until he died, without any chance for being baptised, and if Paradise means Heaven or a state of happiness, he was saved." He acknowledged that it looked as if it was so. The subject never was mentioned again, and we parted as friends, while he expressed a desire for my welfare.

Perhaps it was the first evening after we started down the river, a youth came to me about sunset and asked for a small sum of money, which I handed to him without thinking or asking what he wanted with it, but was hardly gone from me when I thought of his object and felt that I had done wrong, having no doubt that he intended to spend it for intoxicating drinks, which I knew was kept on the boat. Perhaps on the day following one of the young boatmen almost forced me to share in their dinner. I had hardly begun when I thought of his object and left, but he afterwards came to me for money to get a dram with. I said I did not use it myself nor would I furnish means to get it for others. He plead earnestly for it. I told him if it was anything he really needed and that was for his good, I would cheerfully help him to it. I told him of its effects upon the mind and body, health and property, mind and character, and upon society &c., till he acknowledged the evil and almost promised to refrain from it; but I saw that he had no relish for my company and conversation afterward.

A short time afterward, I saw lying on the cabin floor a stout looking man, into whom the evil spirit had entered, and thrown and held him down in a state of unconsciousness, affording a most loathsome, sickening, shameful and degrading exhibition of human filthiness and abomination, and furnished a page in the history of intemperance, written in hieroglyphics too plain to be misunderstood. In the presence of my dram drinking friend I could silently and significantly point to this living illustration of the truth of my previous remarks. As I was walking toward the vender of this qualifying spirit, for several paces I looked him in the face. Said he: "What makes you look so straight at me?" I replied that it made me feel very unpleasant to see that man, and I was looking to see how he felt upon the subject; but he made no reply.

Not long after embarking, my companion from Eastport came to me and said he had gained enough since he came on the boat by gaming to pay his passage to St. Louis, and appeared to think that he was doing much better than I. He had in a previous conversation acknowledged the impropriety of gambling, but would not agree to keep himself clear of it. I gave him to understand that I did not covet his fortune, nor begrudge him his lot. We often met and counseled together on the boat.

On the Sabbath as we went up the Mississippi, he came to me with marks of dissatisfaction in his countenance, and requested me to keep watch at a certain place on the boat so that nothing should be cast overboard unseen. Said he, "Some villain has stolen my coat, and I am going to have the boat searched." Said I, "Perhaps this is for the money you got by gambling." The boat was searched, but the coat was not found; but an officer's coat was found which had been stolen. The last I saw of my unfortunate friend, he was hurrying off the boat at St. Louis, and said he was going to have a regular search for his coat.

This was on Tuesday, the 29th of July, one week from the time we had met at Eastport, in Mississippi.

I immediately passed over to the Illinois side, and set out to go to Decatur, intending to set into work as soon as I could get into business in good society. I had been so annoyed with wickedness and profanity, that I felt like getting if possible where I could never hear it again. I thought that from the time I fell in with the soldiers at Tuscumbia, till I left the boat at St. Louis, I had in less than two weeks heard more profane language, than I had heard in all my lifetime before—near fifty years. For hours after leaving the boat, when anything would make a noise or sudden start about me the language of the boatmen would rush into my mind, as the next thing, according to established order.

I had not gone far when, to my surprise, I found a man who justified the southern rebellion, and said the confederacy was contending for nothing but their rights, and thought they would gain them, and also represented them as having been the most successful that far. The first man I met with whose appearance seemed to give him a claim to my confidence, I asked him how far I would have to go before I would get into good society. I think he said ten or fifteen miles; said they were nearly all foreigners in the region where I met him. I think before, or soon after passing Collinsville, while paying my last toll on the plank road, through the window, I saw an old family Bible in the house, and, pointing to it, I asked if there were any people about there who made that book the rule of their lives. The answer was, the man at the next house did: he also wanted a hand to work for him. This was joyful news. I went to his house and told my business. He was a weakly man and wanted help that would take some of the heavy work off his hands. I told him I was not very able for heavy work myself, but was willing to do what I was able, and if I could not give satisfaction I would be willing to be turned off.

After we had conversed for a while, he thought I would hardly be able to do his work, and we concluded to make no engagement. He would have taken my horse and kept it for me, but I thought it would probably be inconvenient for me to get it again. He appeared to take an interest in giving any useful information that he could, and told me where would be a good place to stop for lodging.

Having passed Collinsville and Troy, I lodged thirty miles from Greenville, Bond county. The second day after, on the way to Decatur, before noon, I stopped with an old minister named Hutchinson, who asked many questions and appeared to sympathize much with me and my friends from the south, and expressed the desire that we might get safely together. He detained me with conversation until after dinner. I felt happy and thankful for kind friends and hospitalities. He directed me to a good man who was needing help, but he had concluded not to hire any one that season, but he told me of a good man on my way with whom I could lodge. I accordingly was taken in by him and treated kindly. His wife was of Tennessee, and was acquainted with the people and places that I had known something of in that country. She had been acquainted with my older brother and a cousin, who were college mates and graduates at Washington college, in East Tennessee, A. D. 1819. Here they had family worship, which was quite a treat, and differing much from evening and morning scenes on a steamboat.

We spent the most of the night in conversation. On the next day which was Friday, the 1st of August, I passed and conversed with S. Paisley; went to Hillsborough, a distance of three miles, and wrote a letter of inquiry to Decatur, and returned to Paisley's, and next morning set in to save hay. The next day I attended preaching at Hillsborough at eleven and by candlelight. I worked at hay making till some time in the day on Thursday, when, being unwell, I went to Hillsborough and received a letter from my son, with the intelligence that the company had all got to their destination, and although most of them had been sick, were then able to do some work. I returned and helped to haul in hay. At night and next morning wrote a letter, which I took to the office at Hillsborough, where I bought and made some instruments for working on clocks, having left my instruments for that purpose at home and being in a shoemaker's shop and hearing his prices, as I had followed shoemaking some from my youth, I thought I could make wages at that business. I heard that there was a shoemaker at Irving who was in need of an assistant, and concluded to try to get in with him. I returned to Paisley's and put handles on my new instruments and worked on his clock.

During this time I worked for him I had a cough which I had been subject to for years. He said he thought I would not stand this climate long; my cough reminded him of his brother who had died of consumption. So far as domestic attachments and the comforts of the world were concerned, this was not a very flattering prospect to me in my situation.

While sitting alone one day under a tree in the yard, where I supposed no eye saw me, my family came to me with an unusual force, especially the youngest children. I was for a little season completely overcome of grief. But again self government was restored, and has not entirely failed me at any time since, though the severest trial had not yet come.

On Saturday, the 9th of August, I and Mr. Paisley went together to Hillsborough, and when about to separate he asked me if I would not return with him and attend church there on Sabbath. I chose to go on to Irving, but when there, the man with whom I expected to get into business, would not agree to take me in unless I would stay with him some months; but as I had written to my son for information concerning labor and wages where he was, and was expecting an answer, I was not prepared to make such an engagement. As it was then near night, I put up in Irving, and thinking it was Friday, inquired for places where I could probably get into work, intending to go next day and attend to that matter preparatory to employment during the next week. In the morning I was up at the dawn of day, but being up stairs, I waited for those below to rise. Meantime I took out my diary, and, to my surprise. I discovered that it was the Sabbath. Then I saw the propriety of Mr. Paisley's invitation to attend church. And now the question with me was, What must I do? I did not wish to travel on the Sabbath, but I was at a tavern and expected of course my bill would be higher than at a private house. But notwithstanding my straightened circumstances, I resolved to stay there until Monday, be charged as I might; the Lord would provide. I saw a church there, and thought I would probably have an opportunity of hearing preaching, and if an opportunity offered, might take a part in public services.

To this time no one in that country knew that I ever exercised in public. Having decided in my mind what course to pursue. I went down and in due time inquired after the church arrangements for the day, but the inn keepers could tell me nothing definite about it; they thought there was going to be Sabbath school that morning at the church, and directed me for further information to a family who, they said, were members of it.

Having obtained the necessary information I went to Sabbath school, was invited to take a part in the reading and answering of questions in a Bible class, when I was astonished at their questions and answers, till a man came in, who gave an interesting lecture upon the observance of the Sabbath and the advantages of Sabbath schools. Before he was through the bell rang for preaching.

At the close of the exercises, as there was no appointment for the evening, I asked one who appeared to be a leader if they would accept of an appointment for a stranger to address them that evening. He said they would gladly, and the appointment was published, and the word got out that a refugee from the south was going to address the people, and considerable of a congregation assembled in eager expectation of hearing a refugee, and no doubt expected to hear much about things in the south, and honored me with the best of attention till I had finished my remarks, and were yet not satisfied.

My clothing was home manufacture. made by my own family, and as the weather was warm I had gone to meeting without my coat. I introduced myself to the congregation by remarking that my appearance before them that day was rather singular, but if they knew the circumstances under which I had come there, they would be more disposed to pity than to blame. But as it was more consistent with the office I filled and the example of Him whom I professed to serve, to seek the happiness of others than to excite sympathy for myself, I would say to them as he said to those who bewailed and lamented him as he was going to be crucified: "Weep not for me but weep for yourselves and your children." And he said to Peter, when he went to wash his feet, "What I do thou knowest not now, but shall know hereafter." So the full import of what I say you may not understand now, but may find out hereafter. Then I went through with the appropriate exercises, without referring, so far as I can recollect, in a single instance, to the political condition of the country. I felt that I was aided in effort; I saw evidence that others felt the same, whether very correctly or otherwise.

The minister who addressed them in the forenoon remained for the evening exercises, and appeared to feel deeply on subjects hinted at in the discourse. Some of the people were greatly disappointed because I had told them nothing concerning things in the south, and wished me then to add that to my discourse. I refused, saying that was not the proper business of the day. They replied that at such a time they thought it was proper to do it. I said I did not feel at liberty to do it; we had had two discourses that day upon subjects proper for us to occupy our thoughts upon, and, with that, we ought to be satisfied; and when I would not, on that day, comply with their wishes, they wished me to do it the next day. I said I did not know that I had anything to relate that would be of any real benefit to them; that I was on expense and did not wish to be detained. One person said it would not cost me anything if I would give them a discourse; I could go and stay with him. So I agreed to meet them the next night, and the appointment was published accordingly. I took the man at his offer, and went and remained with him till Monday morning. I then set out and returned in the evening to Irving without success. But hearing of a man a mile and a half or two miles distant who was wanting help, I set off to see, but was overtaken and detained some time by a storm of wind and rain, so that by the time I got to see the man sought for and arrangements made for business, and was ready to start for my appointment, it was sundown; and as I had traveled all day without feeding, went on foot; and by the time I got to the place for speaking the people were coming out to leave. "Old man," said some of the crowd, "what does this mean? Why were you not here sooner? You must give an account of yourself." I said if they would go back into the house a was ready to do all that, and to fulfill my promise. They went back. As I was going into the house I heard one say, "There he is now, so drunk he can't walk steady." Accordingly, I told the cause of being so late; then gave a brief sketch of my calling and manner of life, to show them that they could not reasonably expect me to go into an extensive and detailed account of things in the country I had left. I then made a brief statement of important facts that I knew as such, and things that I had by report, as rumors that I would not be responsible for the truth of.

As there was a number who expected soon to start for the army, I intended the best part of my discourse to be devoted to their benefit, but as it was late I had to be brief. When I thought I was through, a voice proceeding from the crowd said : "We would like to know how you got away from the south." Said I, "If the people are willing to be detained that much longer, they can have that also." Many voices responded, "Let us have it," so I added that to the account.

I had the fortune to be lodged near the church, and was at my post in the morning in time to meet my engagement, where I worked two days at a threshing machine, till I was entirely overdone. The day following I helped to haul a stack of oats. This I stood tolerably well. The next day I worked on a clock at Irving.

Being disappointed by not receiving a letter as I had expected, and fearing that it was in consequence of something serious, I set out next day for Decatur, and traveled most of
—11

the day through prairies, where I was terribly annoyed with flies; and often as I looked over those vast natural meadows, thought of the speeches I had heard in Alabama the summer before, concerning northern men wanting to take the land in the south for foreigners and free negroes. There was space enough to colonize thousands, on what I thought far better land than most of Alabama.

Owing to a previous recommendation, I lodged that night at Mr. Vermilion's, with whose convorsation and family order I was much entertained and highly delighted. In the morning he made me welcome to remain over Sabbath and attend church with him, free of cost. I acknowledged the generosity, but owing to a conscientious prejudice, declined the favor, and went a few miles to a church of United Presbyterians, where they had Sabbath school but no appointment for preaching that day. I introduced myself and proposed preaching in the evening, which was agreed to, but hearing that there was an appointment for a farewell sermon to be delivered net many miles from there that evening I objected to having an appointment that would conflict with it, and said I would prefer attending it and have none of my own; so the conclusion was to have a discourse at the close of Sabbath school, and to attend the other appointment in the evening.

After my discourse, I was solicited to have an appointment on the following day, to address the people on the state of the country, especially of the south. I excused myself, as I had made my calculations to be near Decatur the next day. I was kindly entertained by Mr. Wadell. We attended the evening appointment, and it was again proposed to me to make an appointment. If I would, was promised as many attendants as could hear me. But I still declined the honor, having no desire to become popular in a political line.

The evening and morning was spent pleasantly, and I was pleased with the society which I had found.

The next day my host accompanied me several miles, and my ideas of the new country were considerably elevated. That day I passed through much good country, and that evening fell in with some acquaintances from the south, in the neighborhood of Mount Zion, southeast of Decatur, just four weeks from the time we had started from Tuscumbia. They had nearly all been sick, but, with the exception of one, who had a fever, were able for some business.

After visiting several places during the following day, to see the friends and relatives from Mississippi, and to get advice for the sick, I lodged with Mr. Bell, where I remained the next day with the sick, and prepared a letter to send home. After making, so far as I could, the necessary arrangements to get the letter conveyed to and through the confederate lines to its place of destination, the next thing was to try to get into some regular employment.

CHAPTER VII.

FIRST FALL AND WINTER'S EXPERIENCE IN THE NORTH.

For this purpose I made an engagement with a man to work on a farm, by the month, and was to set in with him in a short time. I then went and chopped a few days at a sawmill, at which some of the Mississippi boys were working, but some had left on account of the wickedness that prevailed there. I felt a deep interest in keeping our company from being scattered and exposed to bad company and tried to give the best advice I could under existing circumstances. There some of the boys had a little house and boarded themselves.

When I had cut and put up four and a half cords of wood I went to work on the farm, but was disappointed. My employer had taken in a man with a family, and had no use for me. I then went where my son was employed and we repaired a clock, and after looking around for other employment, returned to the mill. As it was thought I could not stand to work out through the winter, I went to Decatur to get into business in a shoe and boot shop, but failed in consequence of an expected draft. I then went and worked about ten days on a farm. And on the 11th of September, went to work in a shoe shop in Decatur. Sadly annoyed with profane language from my boss, and when in a friendly manner I spoke to him of the impropriety of unnecessary words which he used, he took it unkindly and turned upon me swine like, to rend my feelings with ridicule, scorn and blasphemy.

Being informed of a man at Tacusa who was wanting a shop mate, I took passage on the next evening train and landed at Tacusa after dark and found the employer sick. I then inquired for work on a farm, and learned where help was wanted and good wages offered, and was the next morning in time to do a day's work.

The next day, being the Sabbath, I preached at Tacusa. My engagement was to break stubble land, which I continued to do till stopped by rain. I then saw the shoemaker, and found I would not suit him. I then resolved that when my time was out on the farm, if my friends thought it advisable, I would set up a shop of my own and board myself.

My employer now wanted me to help to save prairie hay. I objected, and said it was not in our contract, that I was not able to stand that kind of work. He said it was not very hard. I thought I had experience enough to be a competent judge. But he insisted till I yielded to his wishes, and helped two days, saving and delivering hay. Then came the Sabbath; but as I was suspected of being a spy I had no invitation to preach, and remained at the house of my employer. The night before I had commenced dreaming, which with me is commonly an indication of bad health; the night following I had strong premonitions of approaching sickness. In the morning I told my dream, and said I was going to be sick. I went to work as usual, but before we had finished putting our load on the wagon, I was taken very sick with bilious derangement, violent vomiting, and had to be waited on for some time before I could finish the load, and when I drove into the scales for weighing, I slipped down and crept into the station house, and lay on the sacks of grain till evening, when I saw a wagon that was to pass the house of my employer. I got leave to stretch myself on the bottom of the same, and thus took conveyance to my late house, where, from choice, I took my bed on the floor till some time the next day.

From what I had witnessed in the family, I thought them unskillful nurses of the sick, and the prospect was that I was going to be very sick. But I thought I probably would be able to go on the evening train to Decatur, in the neighborhood of which I had acquaintances who had some skill in such diseases. I also saw the family were uneasy, who spoke of their want of skill and means. I proposed going to the depot—they were fearful I was not able, but were heartily willing if I could go safely. I resolved to risk it, and was conveyed to the station, where were some refugees from Mississippi, who had arrived there the Saturday before, but I was too unwell to have much conversation with them, which, to me, was very desirable, Being very much pained I applied to a physician for something to give relief. The remedy, contrary to expectation produced vomiting, removed some bilious matter and thereby effected a transitory relief.

I hoped that when the train came I could have a chance to lie down and have an easy ride; but, to my disappointment, when I entered the car, I could scarcely get room to *sit* down, and thus, as best I could, had to sit till conveyed to Decatur, and then to walk and carry my clothing from the depot to town, where I lodged.

On the following day, while waiting for conveyance into the country, my sufferings were so intolerable at times, that I about despaired of being able to get away. A doctor gave me a dose of medicine, after the taking of which I obtained relief, and was brought to a lively sense of the worth of health, freedom from suffering, and of my unmindfulness of and a want of gratitude for daily blessings and comforts, and soon began to feel an inclination to sleep. I obtained medicine and directions for treating my case, and was conveyed near to a house at which I was kindly treated. And while resting upon a comfortable bed, was lead to feel thankful for what I enjoyed; and, especially, when I remembered that for want of it many a soldier languished and died among strangers, away from home.

By the next week I was able to ride around and make arrangements for setting up a shop of my own. To accomplish this I had to borrow money from the boys, to be able to get things necessary to furnish a shop for work, and board. I was tired of wandering homeless and in the way about other people's houses, and wished to have a home of my own, where I could have something according to my own notions of propriety; and as my son was not stout, I feared he would have an uncomfortable way of getting through the winter, I thought if necessary I might be able in that way to take him in. And it so turned out that before I was quite ready to go to housekeeping he was taken sick, and the man for whom he was working then wished him to leave. He having heard what I had been preparing for, came to find a home with me.

On the 11th of October we took up our residence in a , near Mount Zion church and seminary, sometimes working in our shop and sometimes at other employments, the remainder of the fall and winter.

This place had been recommended to me as being in the best society in the state, (when perhaps sixty or eighty miles off), and before I was aware that I had got to the favored place, I had made arrangements for wintering there, where I found many worthy old people and some choice families. But, alas! the children were too much left to themselves in too many instances to be much credit to themselves or honor to their parents; and such was the language used on the playground and around the shop where I worked that I honestly thought sometimes I would not have a family of children brought up there for the best estate in the country.

Again, I was mortified to see the jealousy and prejudice that prevailed among the people of that country, a number of whom appeared to entertain a high opinion of their own superior talents and attainments, and while they looked down upon others as quite below, exposed their own nakedness, even to persons of ordinary minds and superficial observation, and to see the people both of church and state have more zeal for names and parties than for the general good of the people.

I had few appointments for preaching during my stay there, and mostly under unfavorable circumstances. A number of Sabbaths passed in view of a church without preaching, while seasons of sadness and depression of spirits rolled on. During the winter I became so afflicted with rheumatism, that I was much disqualified for business, so that though I worked late, I could not in the day and half the night do a good day's work. I purchased corn and had the use of a stable near by for the use of my horse, so that I could make speedy trips when I went out on business.

During the winter and spring I restored most of the idle clocks to their office in the surrounding country. The most of our refugee company wintered and boarded themselves in two small houses near their daily labor. We occasionally saw each other, and our design was, if we could not return to our former home, to select some suitable place and colonize together. We saw enough to impress us deeply with the importance of good society to live in, and this was sadly lacking in many places in this state where some of us had been. The Sabbath was not generally observed as it was in the community we had left. Morals very different and family government out of use. As we could get no news from home, and we saw accounts of outrages being committed on Union people in the south, and of women and children being in a suffering condition, it was thought that some measures should be taken to know the condition of those whom we had left. We had learned that a regiment of Union soldiers, mostly from Alabama and Mississippi, was being made up at Corinth. I being the oldest and most extensively acquainted, it was resolved that I should go on that business. I had determined to quit the shop and try my fortune at clock repairing, so soon as roads would get in order for traveling. As I had made very little during the winter, I was in need of money to pay my way south; so I made arrangements for leaving the shop about the first of April.

By this time our little flock was scattered into two or three counties, wherever they could get suitable employment. I wished to see all if I could before going south, as I then indulged a hope that I would get home in the summer and not return north. According to previous arrangement, leaving my son to close our business at Mount Zion, I started on the 1st of April, 1863, to work on clocks and make a farewell visit among my friends. I found a number of clocks out of order in and about Cerro Gordo, where I remained till the next week. There I spent the Sabbath with interesting society that reminded me of home. I attended Sabbath school and sermon with them in the morning and preached in the evening, having the company of a nephew part of the day.

Having finished my work in that neighborhood, I went to Bennett, in Piatt, and thence to Monticello, where, as I supposed, I heard of two nephews, at a place about ten miles northwest. There I arrived after sunset on Saturday, and found one nephew instead of two at T. E. Bendurents, with whom I attended church on Sabbath, and remained till Monday.

On my way back to Monticello, while stopping to work on a clock, I found the other nephew whom I expected to find at Mr. B's, neither of which knew where the other was. I think I found them wandering as sheep without a shepherd, and prepared the way for them to get together. At the close of the week I was again in the neighborhood of Cerro Gordo, and there with my friends attended church on Sabbath. On the 20th I returned by where my son was at work, and leaving him to dispose of our shop property I visited Decatur and Mount Zion and my good friend Bell. On the next morning, the 21st of April, I started to go south and repaired clocks by the way. On the 23d I was happy to spend the night with a son of a Rev. Mr. Gray, with whom I had been acquainted many years before in Mississippi, and on the 24th at D. Etmire's, was taken sick in the fall. From there I visited some refugees from Mississippi, and received a letter from a Mr. Thompson, directed to H. H. Jennings, Post Provost Clerk, at Vanceller's office, Corinth, Mississippi.

On Saturday night I fell in at Wadell's, where I remained till morning and attended church on Sabbath. On the following Tuesday evening after dusk, I called for lodging at a house where, after telling what was my occupation and reasons for calling for lodging, the landlord remarked that, from the business I followed, he supposed I saw a great many people, and asked me if I heard much said about the war. I replied that at some places I heard something said about it and at others it was not mentioned at all. I said I had heard some news in Taylorville that day that I would like to know the truth of, though it was thought to be reliable, as it had come in the papers two days in succession.

When I had told what the news was, (which was of disaster to the confederates), nothing more was said for some time, but I heard a heavy breath or two escape from them. I thought I knew how their politics went, which was soon expressed in unmistakeable language, charging all the calamities and disasters of the war on Lincoln, and laying down the *negro* as the foundation stone of the whole fabric. He said so many hard things of the administration that I gave him to understand that I thought his charges were rather too heavy; and as he had been speaking unconstitutional acts, I remarked that I made no claims to being a politician, or to know very much about those matters, but I knew a great many were complaining of the constitution being violated, but I acknowledged I was ignorant and did not know wherein it was done, and asked him to inform me of some instances where it had been done. He said Lincoln's whole administration was a violation of the constitution. As I could not understand to my satisfaction how that could be, the old lady took the case into her hands and expressed a suspicion that I was a friend to Lincoln, and said if I was that I had come to the wrong place. I replied that I did not know that he had ever done me any harm, or that I had any right to be his enemy. She said he had done everybody harm in this government, and if she had known I was that kind of a man I should not have staid there, for she had said that no man who was a friend to old Abe should stay in her house. I said if she did not wish me to stay there, all she had to do was to say so and I would leave. She said I could not get to stay anywhere else in that neighborhood. I said I knew I could, if she did not wish me to stay there jut to say so; but she did not venture to say it, but continued to annoy me with her clamor about the negroes, saying that old Abe was a great deal better to the negroes than to the soldiers; that he had the negroes riding on horses, and the soldiers walking and carrying their knapsacks and blankets; and how much more of this kind I cannot now tell. She said the negroes were where they ought to be; they would do no good anywhere else. If they were free they would do no good, but would be a great deal worse off than they are. They were made to be servants, and that was their proper place, &c.

I asked her to prove her doctrine. She said she could do it by the Bible, and took a Bible down with a place marked in it, and handed it to me to read the prooof for myself; and turning away, said: "The servants they had in old times were black." Said I, "You must prove that." She, turning back, said: "Well, if you will not believe the Bible I will put it up," and took it and laid it back on the shelf. I said it did not matter, for I perhaps knew as well what was there as she did.

While she was railing against Lincoln, and against believing and doing things just because Lincoln said so. I replied that it was not Lincoln that said, "Thou shalt not speak evil of the ruler of thy people." She took the notion that I was an abolitionist, and also said she expected I was one of those men who had run away from the south to keep out of the army. Said I, "If I am, what of it?" "You ought to be sent back and made to fight for your country," was the answer. I asked if it would not be hard to have to fight for what we believed to be wrong.

After a while I had leave to retire for the night, and was happy to be alone. Next morning, while at breakfast, I was entertained, or rather annoyed, with a long detail of what had been done in the south, till patience failed, and I said I did not need instruction upon that subject for I had lived in the south; I knew for myself what was done there, and perhaps knew some things that they knew nothing about. I knew that previous to the presidential election calls were made and volunteers were obtained professedly for the express purpose of preventing Lincoln from taking his seat at Washington. Said I, "What do you think of that?" The old lady said she did not know whether that was so or not. I said I was aware that some people were not willing to believe the truth when they heard it, and there the subject dropped.

When I asked the landlord his charge, he said: "Go to the old woman." When I asked her she said a dollar. This was for a bed, a breakfast and feed for my beast; for supper I had, and my beast fed before going there. The common charge there for a man and a horse's supper and breakfast was fifty cents. She said if I had been the right sort of a man she would not have charged me anything. She also said she had two beds in her room, and she put abolitionists in one and other people in the other, and she had put me in the abolition bed. I said she charged me more than any one else had since I had been in the state, and I thought she had no right to it; but if she could ask it, I could give it. I said it was hard, but light in comparison with some other things; and I was well forewarned that I had hard things to bear, but had the comforting assurance that they should work together for my good. And as to being the right sort of a man, that was what I had been aiming to be; and if I had been so ignorant and unfortunate as to be what I had aimed not to be, she ought to pity rather than blame me. This was at Funderburg, in the neighborhood of Taylorville, Christian county. The lesson I there learned was probably worth many times its cost. I afterwards used precaution, so as not often to stop where I was likely to be snakebitten.

On Thursday the 30th, which by the President had been appointed for a day of fasting and prayer, I attended church in Hillsborough, Montgomery county, and spent the evening with S. Paisley, where I had done my first work in the state. On Saturday evening, the 3d of May, I stopped within six miles of Carlisle, where I remained until Monday.

On Saturday night I heard of strange things as they were

thought, being done by spirit-rapping. Next day till noon, I spent in a grove near by, reading. After dinner some of the wonder workers came in, and were performing in a different part of the house from where I was engaged in reading. Norman, the landlord, asked me to go and witness their performance. I did not wish to go, but yielded to his importunities and witnessed their performance, and saw them, if I am not deceived, trying to deceive others by doing themselves what they attributed to an invisible spirit. They had a table beating time to music, answering questions and confirming propositions by a specified number of raps upon the floor. While it was performing, some three or four girls were sitting with their hands on it, and Norman caught hold of it and put his weight most on it, when, from the position of their bodies and the swelling of the muscles in their arms and shoulders, I would have thought they were making great exertions, but they denied it all, and the table was silenced.

The girls then said it was not to be expected that the spirit would perform while he was acting in such a manner. He replied: "It is a poor spirit that is not stronger than I am." It was asked if the spirit there had ever inhabited a human body: if it had ever been at the moon, &c. I was filled with disgust and abhorrence, though I said nothing.

It was requested that I should answer some questions. I refused. They insisted, till I told them there was one question they might ask; that was, if the spirit there was a Divine spirit. The Bible, which I held in my hand, was dictated by it. It was given by the inspiration of a holy and unchangeable Spirit, whereby the rules there laid down were given to men. I then repeated some of the commandments, the institution of the Sabbath, and repeated a part of the 58th chapter of Isaiah, with regard to its proper observance, and asked if it was reasonale to suppose that the Holy Spirit would give answers to questions proposed by persons, when they were going contrary to, and trampling upon those rules.

The medium spoke up in defense of their conduct, and said they had been singing good songs, and she thought that was a very proper exercise on the Sabbath. I said if it was done according to the dictates of the Spirit, it was all right. If they would sing with the spirit and with the understanding, but there was reason to fear that people too often sang without caring or thinking of the meaning of the words, or of honoring God; but for their own pleasure, because it is that for which they have a natural relish.

I also said I was reminded of what the Spirit taught would be in the latter days, for it expressly says that in the last days men shall be lovers of their own selves and of pleasure more than God. That wicked men shall wax worse and worse, deceiving and being deceived; that the coming of Christ shall be after the working of Satan, with all power, and signs, and lying wonders, and deceiveableness of unrighteousness. They soon after took occasion to leave.

The week following, having passed through Clinton, Washington and Perry counties, and crossed Muddy river, in Jackson county, into a hilly and heavily timbered country, where was no more prairie.

On Saturday I stopped at South Pass, in Union county, where I remained till Monday. On Sabbath I attended preaching in a grove, where they had a funeral sermon preached, the sacrament administered and their feet washed. I was delighted with their music, as it was more soft and harmonious than anything of the kind I had heard in the state, and reminded me of what I had heard in better days. Why it was that they made so many jars and discords in music in so many places where I had been, I could not tell, unless it was because every one felt competent to lead, and did not regard any one as common leader.

The manner in which female voices were sometimes used reminded me of the screaming and squalling of cats, fowls and wild animals, and was more like the strong wind that rent the mountain and broke the rock to pieces, than the still small voice that accompanied the presence of the Lord, and unlike the soft, harmonious church melody that corresponds with the harmonious spirit of angels, and of the just made perfect.

>Such spirits filled with love divine,
>   As incense sweet to God incline;
>Inflated thus they upward rise,
>   To seats of bliss beyond the skies.

Again I pursued my way towards Cairo, sometimes delighted with the scenery by the way, and sometimes feeling as if things were going unfavorably with me, and sometimes rejoicing to see that they were for the best at last. For instance: On Wednesday the 13th, after traveling a part of the day in the rain, as my custom was, when I heard of any work in my line by the way, to attend to it, I left the road to do some work at a house where some refugees were at work. My job here proved to be a failure, and having paid for dinner and horse feed, I went on my way, feeling that I had been spending my time for no benefit; but stopping to talk some with those refugees, I learned that at the next house on my way, and where a clock was out of order a refugee was staying, with whose name I was well acquainted. I went to the house and found, as I expected, that he was the son of a man whom I had known from my boyhood. He was from Alabama. This was a joyful meeting. He requested me to remain some days, and McMurrey, with whom he was staying, was pleased to have me do so.

As I wished to leave my horse in that country till I went south, there I found an opportunity for doing so, and again felt that all was for the best. A request was made that I should remain and preach on the next Sabbath, and it was thought I could get plenty of work for several days. Though I then thought I was nearly clear of rheumatism, my general health was declining, and I complied with their request—fixed up a few clocks, wrote to my son and on Sabbath preached at 11 o'clock and at candle light

On Monday, the 18th, I went on a train to Villa Ridge to Cairo. Furnished myself for the trip, and on the steamer Ruth took passage to Memphis, where we landed at 11 P. M. Tuesday, and remained on board until morning.

In the morning I obtained a pass from the provost marshal. The morning train being gone I did not start for Corinth until the next morning, after undergoing the required examination. While stopping at a station by the way, a youth, who could not speak better English than I could, myself being the judge, came to me and in an impudent manner, as I thought, said I had to be searched. I asked why that should be done, as it had been done before I entered the car. He said he was informed by telegraph and knew the day before that I was coming. I asked where and from whom it came. He did not tell, but said it was from some of my friends. I said I doubted it. He said it was from some who were better friends to their country than I was. I told him I doubted that too, and if he had heard anything of the kind, he had probably got it from a copperhead. He denied it, but said I had to be examined, that it might be known what I had with me. I submitted to the claim.

A short time before I had taken a little book out of my pocket, containing a list of names of persons for whom I had worked, and with whom I had lodged, to let a soldier see if any of them were persons with whom he was acquainted. We left our seats for the accommodation of others, and in doing so, dropped my book without knowing it. While I was being examined and was showing what I had with me. when I went to show my little book, I could not find it. The examiner said he did not have it. I said I had it just before he came, and I could prove it. A youth stepped up to us and asked what was lost. On being told, he presented the book, which but for this circumstance would have been lost.

The examination soon ended; then said I: "Sir, you have examined me, now show your authority for what you have done." Said he: "Do you think I have none?" "I think it doubtful," said I. He said he had none to show, but there was an officer in another car who could bear witness of the fact, and asked if I wished him brought. Said I: "If you have any authority let it be seen." He left, and again returned with a man who said the other had the right to search me and to have me stopped and searched if he chose. Said I: "If he had the authority it is all right." But whether he had the right or not, I never knew.

An officer who had been absent and was returning to his post at Corinth, having heard and seen the foregoing, seated himself by me and commenced a conversation concerning my home, country, acquaintances, &c. He said there was one of their boys in the car who I probably was acquainted with, and told his name. I thought I knew him or his father. I found him to be one of my acquaintances, who had left home some time after I did.

Again I was lead to notice with admiration how unpromising occurrences brought about most gratifying and beneficial results. This was a soldier of the first Alabama cavalry, then stationed at Glendale. He while on a scout, had got separated from his company, and had to take a circuitous rout to get back. We had passed from Columbus, Ky., to Memphis on the same boat, and from Memphis in the same car, and did not recognize each other, till this occurrence introduced us. By him I received the first information concerning my family, and was happy to learn that our people had not been mistreated, and that, though they had been threatened with confiscation, all had passed harmlessly away.

He also told of several others of our acquaintances, who were at Corinth and Glendale, and I then had a guide to the different points I wished to visit. Along the way a large portion of the country was lying desolate; fields without fences, houses vacant and no stock of any kind to be seen about those waste places. Some of the houses were occupied by soldiers.

At one of the stations we learned that one of the pickets had been killed the night before, and one or two taken from their posts, and it was thought the train was likely to be fired into that day. As several soldiers and officers were on the train, they were put in readiness to meet an attack, if made. We got through to Corinth about sunset and delivered Thompson's letter to Jennings, and with my new companion lodged at the Soldiers' Home.

CHAPTER VIII.

OCCURRENCES AT CORINTH AND GLENDALE.

Next morning we set off for Glendale, ten miles east of Corinth, and neither of us being stout we had to stop and restoccasionally by the way, through a country abounding with enemies. Late afternoon we arrived at camp, where I met with friends, from whom I learned something concerning my friends and kindred and the state of things in their country.

While in camp I had my abode with a mess of soldiers, in which was one who had lived at my house, and had been there long after I had left, and gave an account of a distressing time of sickness in that neighborhood, and a number of deaths. Among the deceased of my relations was a brother, a sister and two neices, daughters of my only surviving brothers, and a daughter of my own.

In some families nearly all had been sick. Such was the case with my own, and some were very near dying, and my oldest died.

> When all these things to me were told,
> What deep emotions through me thrilled,
> As if the blood ran through me cold,
> And deep within the soul was chilled.
>
> How sad the picture fancy drew,
> Of those from whom I had to stay,
> While they such scenes were passing through,
> Till some by death were called away.
>
> Their dying features came to view,
> And scenes of last expiring breath,
> And chilly sweat their cheeks bedew,
> As they unconscious sink in death,

*—12

Their glassy eyes did upward roll,
  As if to take a long farewell
Of their released, departed soul,
  No more together there to dwell.

The mortal strife is through at last,
  To be renewed again no more;
Cold Jordon's waves all over pass'd,
  To other scenes beyond the shore.

Now, Oh my God, may I indulge
  The wish, a thing so dear to know,
That thou to me would this divulge,
  That they are free from sin and woe.

True, in the church they had a name,
  And did some honor in that place;
If now on high they have the same,
  To them secured by saving grace,

Oh, how my soul would then rejoice,
  My heart with inward pleasure swell,
And I with joy could raise my voice,
  A Savior's wonderous works to tell.

What troubles I could then out-brave,
  Above those fleeting sorrows rise,
Nor let the solemn, silent grave,
  One mournful tear draw from mine eyes.

But if there is a different state,
  To which the unbelieving go,
It now with them is quite too late,
  The peaceful way of life to know.

Nor can they profit by thy grief,
  Or all that friends can undergo,
Nor yet obtain the least relief,
  By those with whom they fain would go.

The case we must submit it now,
  To Him whose ways are just and right,
And in submission humbly bow,
  For so it seemed good in his sight.

The day after my arrival at Glendale, I went around and saw a number of my acquaintances, some of whom were sick. As their regiment was not full they had no chaplain. I was advised to go to the general and make arrangements for being appointed chaplain of their regiment. This I was inclined to do if my health would enable me properly to fill the place; but of this I was doubtful.

The day following being Sabbath, as there was little opportunity during the day, I preached to the soldiers at night. It was distressing to witness the wickedness that prevailed in camp. The day following I went to the general's office at Corinth, and read the law with regard to the qualification and appointment of chaplain. While there I mailed letters to friends in Illinois with all the information that I could collect from home. I again returned to Glendale in poor health, and devoted part of the time to visiting the sick. This, I found was injurious to my health. I had enjoyed the pleasure of hearing from friends at home, but was informed that they had received no account of us. The next thing to be sought for, was some medium by which information could be communicated to them; but I found there was no communication by mail; and if a private person was found by the confederates carrying a letter from north to south, though from husband to wife, death was the penalty. As men were there who had served in the confederate army, and were then serving in the Union army, who I saw and conversed with, and who had been caught with dogs by the confederates to compel them to aid in their cause; and as there were families, parts of families and individuals coming to the Union lines from the south every few days, under circumstances which confirmed a shocking tale of dreadful and desperate deeds, I could not doubt the danger of one losing his life if caught with a letter, and under such circumstances I could not ask a person to carry one for me; so that I almost despaired of conveying any information to them concerning us.

But as people were frequently passing privately from the Union lines to a section of country from fifteen to twenty miles from my home, and as one was going soon to a neighborhood where I was acquainted, I wrote the following acrostic, perhaps not verbatim, as I kept no copy of the first, which I supposed those acquainted with what it referred to would understand; but those who were not, one of a thousand would not be likely to understand anything about it, and no one would be damaged for carrying it.

It was intended to show who the writer was, the person addressed and who from, and that the rest of our company were alive and well, and to inspire to hope and confidence in God.

*Larephath's scenes again revive,
†Elijah's God will still contrive.
Forever be his name adored,
Eternal King, Almighty Lord.

Endles as are His countless days,
May we show forth His worthy praise;
Still trusting to His faithful word,
That needed help He will afford.

Each grief and we drive far away,
Restore the peace for which we pray;
Though tears the face may oft bedew,
Old aunts, uncles growing few.

My firstling gone and Nancy too,
And other plants that near them grew,
Removed from time and mortal care,
You where their ancient fathers are.

Away from strife and war unjust,
Returning to their mother dust,
Entombed beneath the silent clod,
Their spirits all returned to God.

As round their ancient parents nigh,
Those plants did sicken droop and die,
Those far from home and native land,
In life and health and vigor stand.

Those eyes that are as burning lamps,
Light guarding hosts that round encamps
The face that shines bright as the sun,
Directs the race that they must run.

Will be their help, and sun and shield,
While they to Him their service yield.
As He hath said in days of old.
No good from them will He withhold.

Now one thing more I here must tell,
Then bid my friend a long farewell,
This little song was first brought round,
‡Near where St. Paul Aquila found.

This was written on the 29th of May, and read and explained to some of my friends and the bearer, who all thought it would completely answer the purposes for which it was written. It was given to a man to carry as his own proper-

---

* 1Kings, XVII, 9.   †2 Kings, I, 14.   Acts, XVIII, 1, 2.

ty, to be committed to faithful hands, who would convey it to my family, with verbal instructions to show it to my oldest brother, if they did not understand it. I have since been informed that they heard of it, but did not receive it.

I remained about the camp during the week and furnished wood to do the cooking for the mess with whom I stayed, and frequently carried water, and often pitied the soldiers who had to be out day and night on a scout, and often came in tired, sleepy and hungry, and then had to cook their provisions. On Saturday night and Sabbath I preached to them again.

The weather being damp, things about camp were in a condition well calculated to produce sickness. I thought of boarding at some house inthe neighborhood, from which I could visit the soldiers, and especially the sick, every day. But this was thought unsafe, as the secesh were slipping around, and doing mischief when they had an opportunity, I would be liable to fall into their hands. As I thought I could not stand it long to be all the time confined in the unhealthy atmosphere of the camp and hospital, I went to Corinth to get into employment there, and commenced work for a man who put me to dressing undried pine plank, where I was exposed to the scorching sun. I had a very annoying cough, and being thus exposed made it worse.

After noon my employer said I was not fit to work, and paid me for a half day's labor, and I returned to Glendale and again preached to the soldiers. As the weather was damp and sometimes stormy, and I sometimes being alone in a damp tent, caught cold, and my health continued to decline, so I was convinced of my inability to perform the duties of a chaplain in the army, and that I would not be justifiable in undertaking it. And as I saw no good ground of hope of getting home before fall, I thought it would be best to return to Illinois, where I could do something for a livlihood, and might do something for the benefit of my family. From what I had seen among the soldiers, there was little chance to hope that I could be of much benefit to them. I thought I had seen profane and wicked men before, but the 1st Alabama cavalry, I then thought, exceeded all for profanity that I had ever known The religious and moral men among them were ashamed of their own country and countrymen, for many of them had no regard for the feelings of any class or profession. While I have been preaching to a

congregation of soldiers, others of them were fiddling and
sporting so near, that I could hear them distinctly; and
some spent the time in card playing, which they continued
till late hours in the night.

I sometimes had occasion to remark, that when persons
who knew my profession, principles and manner of life
would curse and swear in my presence, I had little ground
of hope of usefulness to them. I sometimes thought that
such people would not be permitted to enjoy the benefits of
a peaceable government, if established, though they might
be instrumental in establishing it.

Near Corinth was a large, fenceless field of cotton, cultivated by contraband negroes, mostly women and children,
The road from Corinth to Glendale passed through this field
and some of the Glendale boys thought it their privilege to
tease and perplex those black fools, as they thought them,
some of whom, perhaps, had more sense, and not much less
education, and no worse morals than a number of them,
whose names in wisdom's volume may stand among the lowest class of moral Bedlamites.

Adversity is a good school,
When nothing else will teach a fool.
Calamity subjects to rules
When nothing else will humble fools.

And sure this war with all its pain,
Is but a cure for the insane,
And all the shame, and woe, and grief,
Is to reclaim from unbelief.

Such is the scourge their sins provide,
To humble well a nation's pride,
The lowly raise, the proud bring low,
The wonderous ways of God to show.

And thus convince presumptuous fools,
That God in earth and heaven rules;
And thus his glory brightly shines,
Through wicked schemes for men's designs,

And plainly shows, vain mortals all,
That pride is bound to have a fall,
And make rebellious sinners know
That wickedness will lead to woe.

That which the just from evil takes,
The wicked into shivers breaks.

To those it brings a better day,
While these as chaff are blown away.

The Lord the just will well refine,
That they may all more brightly shine;
From troublings then the wicked cease,
And leave the world to perfect peace.

The righteous then will long be blessed
With happy days and peaceful rest,
Sure once the Lord with mighty flood,
Did make his threats and promise good.

When He from earth all nations swept,
In Noah's ark a seed was kept,
And creatures all from earth erased,
From that old bark were soon replaced.

And those who then the Lord obeyed,
Obtained the promise he had made,
In smoke and vapor, fire and blood,
Of late is heard the voice of God.

Though thousands these may often tell
The prophets' words are faithful still,
And come the promise surely will,
The hope of nations all fulfill.

Though waiting long and anxious quite,
Some hoped and died without the sight,
Though nations many be erased,
And much of earth an empty waste.

In faithfulness to promise true,
New earth and heaven may ensue,
And all the nations God may bless,
And fill the earth with righteousness.

Though man from God and honor fell,
Again the Lord will with him dwell.
Though men on earth the Savior slew,
He here will dwell with them anew.

For in his word this truth appears,
He here shall reign a thousand years.
Dear Savior come with kind relief,
Let joy succeed this time of grief.

On Sabbath, the 7th of June, at a sawmill by the railroad in sight of camp, I preached to a well behaved audience. a number of whom were sharpshooters from the stockade.

This, to me, was encouraging and reviving to my feelings. I also attended prayer meeting that night with sharpshooters and was gratified to know that they met for prayer twice a week.

I remained at Glendale until the next Friday. The weather being disagreeable and changeable, I caught more cold and had a very distressing cough. There was thought to be no safety in those parts, and they were daily looking for an attack from the rebel forces that were lurking around.

On Friday I returned to Corinth and expressed my views to Gen. Dodge, who approved of my plans, and said I would not be safe in going home to live under three years. When I was preparing to leave, the General proposed giving me charge of about sixty women and children, to be conveyed north; but I asked to be excused, as I was poorly able to take care of myself. I was so very unwell, that I had not a moment's rest, so that I could have had very little enjoyment with company. I felt as if disease was preying upon every part of my system. When I went on the cars my lungs were so sensative that I had to keep my face below the windows, to avoid irritation from the action of the atmosphere. The cough and misery in my chest appeared to denote confirmed consumption.

On Saturday evening I arrived at Memphis, where I remained till Monday morning, when, from comfortable lodging, change of diet, and a day's rest, my health was more improved than I had entertained the slightest hope of. While I was there, my host told me if I would write a letter and leave it with him, he thought he could send it to my people. This I did, hoping to give them and others the satisfaction of hearing from me and their friends. But this, also, I have learned was a failure.

I then had to get a pass to Cairo, and a vast number being there on the same business, I had to stand and wait so long, that when the object was obtained, my strength was exhausted, so that I had to sit down and rest on the floor for nearly an hour, to be able to proceed. Late in the afternoon went on boat, twenty-four days from the time I had left there for Corinth. While I was waiting for the boat to leave, two women took a fight on the river bank, opposite a boat crowded with soldiers, who raised a shout that could be heard "*far, far away.*"

As the boat was speeding its way over the rolling tide,

along its pathway of foam, sad was the reflection that I had turned my back again toward home, and those with whom I much desired to be, and the sentence often rose in my mind, "I am going the way whence I shall never return," and I felt as if it probably might be so, for my prospect for many days was not at all flattering. On that night I took a dose of pills, which gave me so much relief that I was convinced that my liver was chiefly at fault.

At Cairo I obtained medicine and went on the afternoon train to Villa Ridge, six miles from McMurrey's, to which place I had to go on foot, but was happy to be where I could sit and rest under a tree by the way without fear. I remained at McMurrey's some days for the improvement of my health, and preached for them on Sabbath ; but as it was a sickly place, and many of the people and some of the family where I was staying were taken sick, I thought it was time to get out of the way, and to seek a more healthful region.

As soldiers at Glendale requested me to inquire in the neighborhood of Anna and Jonesborough for their relatives, and if I found them to write to Glendale concerning them. I accordingly on the 23d of June found one of those refugees from Alabama, and lodged at Parson Hamilton's, near by. It being a rainy time, I remained there some days, and enjoyed christian like order, conversation and kind treatment.

When the weather became more favorable, I went on my way, working on clocks occasionally, till I arrived on Saturday evening at the house of Parson Morris, with whom I stopped and preached in his stead on Sabbath, at Limestone Church. And on Monday set off again in better health than a short time before I had any hope of ever again enjoying, and on the 13th of July I arrived at Morgan's mill, where my son was at work, near Decatur, in Macon county, after an absence of three months.

CHAPTER IX.

TRAVELS AND OCCURRENCES IN THE NORTH.

Though I was again among friends and acquaintances, mine was an unenviable lot: having no home, no certain abiding place nor employment, only as I could find it by wandering from place to place. I realized the truth of Solomon's words : "He that leaveth his place is like a bird that wandereth from its nest." The foxes had holes and the birds of the air had nests, but I had not where to lay my head; and often had to be where my company was not desired, and in society that was very disagreeable to me.

After visiting some of the neighbors, I spent a short time in the neighborhood of Eastman's mill, where some of our company were working, and then started to Springfield to get some articles pertaining to my occupation, but was so nearly out of money that I feared I would have to turn back before reaching the place, but had the fortune to find work occasionally, that enabled me to go forward with my purpose, to the accomplishment of my object.

From Springfield I went to a place, I think, called Pleasant Plains, and made arrangements for preaching there on Sabbath, and went forward with my business in the adjacent neighborhood; and in this excursion passed the residence of the far famed Peter Cartright, whom I would gladly have seen, but passed without the sight.

While working on a clock in this neighborhood, I was annoyed by a woman's talk about the doings of the government, and people wishing to equalize themselves with negroes. She said others might equalize themselves with negroes if they chose, but she would *never*; and held forth the idea that southern people had been wronged, and that the negroes should not have been meddled with. Although I had learned, for the most part, to be quite modest and reserved, on this occasion my patience failed, and I remarked that it looked to me like an insult to common sense for anyone to pretend to vindicate the propriety of the course pursued by the southern people. And as to the people equalizing themselves with the negroes, if they did not do it there to the lowest degree, and in the meanest sense of the word, I did not know where it was done. I told her something of the mixture of the races that existed there, and of slaves resembling their owners, in some cases being whiter; and added that a period was coming when some of the down-trodden negroes would be raised as much above some of the noble white people, as they were then held below them. She said she did not believe it, Said I: "You do not believe the Bible." She said she did. I said I had seen negroes who had given satisfactory evidence that they were good christians, and I supposed she would not deny that there were some bad ones among white people, and the Bible taught us that two characters and two places comprehended and were to contain the whole human family : the one prepared for the righteous, where they shall shine as the sun ; the other for the devil and his angels, where the wicked shall go into everlasting punishment and shame and contempt. The wicked, white and black, shall be abased in one; and the righteous white and black shall be exalted together in the other, unless there are two places for the different colors, of which the Bible gives no account. She intimated that she thought this would be the case. Said I, "If you will give your conscience fair play, and speak your honest convictions upon the subject, you will acknowledge you do not believe it."

 As she no longer did contend,
 This brought the subject to an end,

In my travels I saw many things that betokened evil to the country, and darkened my prospects for the future, and lead me to fear that the days of evil would be many. On Sabbath morning, the common business of the week and topics of the time engrossed the conversation. Gathering blackberries, preserving those that were gathered, and strolling from house to house in the country, was the employment of many for the day.

When I went to the plains I learned that my appointment had not been published, but knew not why, but understood the people there were generally copperheads. I inquired for an agreeable place to stop at till Monday, and was happy to fall in with a family who were spending it in the good old way; all in quietude and composure, with plenty of good books and religious papers to read and the old family Bible, the appearance of which and the place it occupied, gave evidence that it was one honored and highly esteemed in the family, and often applied to for instruction and council. Its instructions were heard at the family altar, at the time of the morning and evening sacrifice.

> To me this was a grateful treat,
> With such I did too seldom meet,
> Such scenes of real and pure delight,
> Where kindred spirits all unite.
>
> Their wants and cares are open spread
> In view of Christ their common Head.
> And all their minds in union run,
> And their's and Christ's, and God's are one.

After doing work round in that section a few days, I worked back to Mount Zion, where I attended church on Sabbath the 2d of August, with several dollars more than when I started to Springfield. My postoffice was at Decatur, where I received communications from Glendale and the south part of Illinois, from correspondents, upon whom I depended for information from home. As I had received an intimation that my wife was talking of trying to come north, I kept the postoffice watched closely to get the first notice, if she should come, of her getting to the Union lines, so as to make the earliest possible arrangement for her transportation to some suitable place for the family. I would take a round now in one and then in another part of the country, and back to the office, till, in this way, I had gone over a part of Macon, Dewitt, Moultrie and Piatt, and had seen most if not all of my friends from Mississippi.

The first round was attended by some remarkable occurrences. About the 8th of August, as I was stopping three nights in succession at the same place, one night I dreamed of a voice addressing me, as from one of my own family, which sounded as familiar as if I had been with them at home. The next night the word "Pa" was addressed to me, as if calling for me, or to attract attention, by a voice so plain and so fully recognized as the voice of one of my own family, that I awoke; and it appeared just as clear and distinct in my mind, and remained, as if it had been a reality.

During this round I sometimes had to travel late before I could get lodging. On the 12th, after traveling until late and without supper, I lodged among the hay in a barn, four or five miles north of Decatur.

While thus I rested in the hay,
Some moments sweetly passed away,

Some pleasure true I there could find,
As Bethlehem was brought to mind,

When in a manger poor and mean,
The Lord a stranger there was seen.

With feelings quite composed and calm,
I thought of him at Bethlehem,

When he on earth began his race,
He had his birth near such a place,

And shepherds there by angels taught,
The Savior found whom they had sought.

And men of wisdom coming far;
Were thither guided by a star.

And to the infant Savior prayed.
And precious gifts and offerings made.

'Mong poor of men and meaner things,
They thus beheld the King of Kings.

If He who reigns in glory high,
Such things could bear, how well may I.

Nor think it shame or loss to me,
To fare like one so great as He,

Nor let one cross reproachful word,
For things like these by me be heard,

Nor ever think myself forgot,
Because like his has been my lot,

Nor think my grief exceeding sore,
When His has been ten thousand more.

Sin He endured and overcame,
By grace secured I'll do the same.

Let Him of earth and sky possessed,
Do with his own what He sees best.

May I submissive to Him bow,
Nor prove unfaithful to my vow.

I continued my course of operations till the 12th of September, when I visited Decatur the last time and began to move eastward, having made enough to meet all demands against me and have a few greenbacks left. As I had relations at Indianapolis whom I had resolved to visit if I could make enough by the way to clear my expenses, having visited my friends and fellow refugees, as some thought for the last time in Illinois, and satisfied their claims against me, on the 18th of September I started from Anderson's in Piatt county, for Indianapolis, Ind., where I arrived on the 28th, and remained a short time with my kindred. There I heard of a cousin of mine living at Greencastle, Ind. I resolved to call upon him on my way to the south part of Illinois, where I had calculated to winter in a milder climate and nearer home, to which I hoped to return in the spring; but if not, provided the country and society suited I might have my family brought there.

Having written to my friends in Illinois, informing them or my designs, I left for Greencastle, where I arrived on the first of October, having a little more than made my expenses. People had so often been imposed upon by clock peddlers, as they generally called them, that they were afraid to risk a stranger any more, and many a clock showed that they had good reasons for being so.

My cousin at Greencastle thought I could get plenty of employment about there for a length of time, and also that he could get me into other business that would be more profitable, and I concluded to remain and see what could be done: so I set in to doing jobs where I could, returning frequently to the postoffice.

As I became better acquainted my business became more profitable, and had it not been that I feared the winter and wished to go south, I perhaps might have done well in that country. My business took me into the families of people of every faith and order, religious and political. I heard their talk and saw their walk, and saw in their families what they were doing for society and for the hope of the country; and though I was thus employed in the state from the 23d of September to the 25th of November, I do not remember to have witnessed family worship but in one family. In many families they neither asked the Lord's blessing nor returned thanks at their tables, though they were members of churches. I attended church every Sabbath but one, heard some good sermons and preached twice during that time; but this fell short of satisfying the inward desire.

The country was divided into two parties: some were called abolitionists and some butternuts, and I understood the women fought about butternut breastpins, and that, too, if I am not mistaken, at church. I aimed to keep clear of political controversy, and as much as possible to live in peace with all men; but sometimes I had to be crafty and evasive to do this, and then could not always succeed. I thought I could generally know a butternut at first sight by his countenance, and did not often find myself mistaken, but often found them cross, disagreeable, fault-finding and frequently ignorant and unreasonable, (though sometimes wiser in their own conceit than seven men who can give a reason,) and were not afraid to speak evil of dignities, but indulged in all manner of hard and evil speeches against that which was intended for the lawless and disobedient, and against rulers and those in authority, for a terror to evil doers.

On one occasion I lodged with a man affected with this malady and Universalism, who professed to be more philanthropic, beneficent and liberal, than those belonging to churches and professing to be religious; but when I paid this bill, it was just double the common charge; while some of those whom he accused of being close-fisted, hypocritical, and giving visible signs of the devil within, had lodged me free of charge; for I found a number who were kind and generous hearted toward the stranger and unfortunate.

In the same neighborhood, as I was after sunset passing for the last time through that section to Greencastle, a man overtook me who had previously invited me to his house to work on a clock, and had disappointed me. He again asked me to go on the same business. I asked if he was joking; he said he was not—his clock was stopped and he wanted it fixed, and wished me to go and do it. He said it would be an hour before he would be there, but I could lodge there and fix his clock, for he would be there in about an hour. I thought that would be preferable to going five or six miles after night. He then asked me to drink with him. I said I never used it except as medicine and on particular occasions. He said it was a particular occasion with him then, and he was going to have a dram.

While he and another man were taking their dram, I went on, but began to feel suspicious that he would get too much under the influence of bottle spirits for his house to be an agreeable lodging place. From this consideration, previous to going there, I went and saw another man in whom I had confidence, and asked his advice in the case. He said if the other had invited me to go, he thought it would all be right, so off I went to fix the man's clock, and notwithstanding I had been delayed a considerable length of time he had not got home; and though I told my business and how I had been induced to go there, the woman appeared afraid to permit me to be about the house in his absence. I said if she feared any disagreeable consequences I would not stay. She asked if I could not lodge in the neighborhood and fix the clock the next day. I said if I did not do it that night I should not do it at all, for I had intended being at Greencastle that night, and to leave the state as soon as I could arrange my business for leaving, and if I did not stay there I would go to Greencastle that night. She did not know where her husband was, nor when he expected to be home. When I described a horse that I had seen at a certain place, she said it was his, and that he staid there more than he did at home, but she thought if he wanted me to fix the clock, if I would go there he would return with me. I went and found him drunk; and not understanding my statements, he showed a disposition to be cross. I said if there was any danger of a misunderstanding between us, I preferred going on my way. He said all would be right, go and fix the clock, and started with me in a hurry.

He said after starting, "You must look over this, I am drinking. Won't you?" I replied, "If there is none to whom you are under no higher obligations than you are to me, you need not trouble yourself about it.

After going a little farther, said he : "I want you to tell me candidly how you stand with the administration." Said I, "In what respect? You must explan yourself." "Are you in favor of Lincoln's administration?" Said I : "We had better get your clock fixed, and defer that to another time." "I want you to tell me just now if you are in favor of Lincoln's administration I have no use for you." Said I : "I don't know that I have a right to find much fault with the old man." He repeated the question at different times, without getting anything more definite upon the subject. When we got to the house he ordered his wife to prepare supper, but could not forget his questions. I tried to get his consent to dismiss the subject until better prepared for profitable conversation, but did not succeed. "What do you think about the negro?" said he " *What* about the negro," said I. "Do you think he ought to be free?" "I have thought that so soon as they were in a condition to be free, so as to promote the interests of both races, it might be well enough to let them be free," was my reply. "Do you think a negro is as good as you are?" came next. I said I supposed some were, and some were not. He added very emphatically and contemptuously: "*Yes, I know* you are no *better* than a *negro*, and I will treat you *like* a negro." I said I expected to treat him with civility, whether he was worthy of it or not. Said he: "Yes, you shall do it, but I will treat you like a nigger. You sha'n't stay in my house tonight. Do you think I would let a man who is no better than a nigger sleep in the house with my family? No! you shall not sleep under my roof. You may fix the clock but you sha'n't stay here." I rose, took my cloak, not thinking of my saddle bags, and said to him, " I shall not ask you to stay." He continued to repeat his assertion. I replied: "I have told you I shall not ask you to stay; but I have stayed in many a better man's house." He rose, raised his chair, as if he was going to strike me, and said: "Say that again, and I will knock you down." Said I: "Once is enough." He ordered me to get out of his house, and followed me, saying, if I did not go faster he would hit me.

I went with a regular step till I had got outside of the yard gate to my beast, without paying any attention to him, he all the time threatening me if I did not go faster and then ordered me to get on my horse and clear out. I did not still obey, but walked some distance to an outside gate, where, turning to my horse, I saw my saddlebags were missing, and went back to the yard fence. He was then talking at a loud and rapid rate to his wife, but hearing my voice he came to the door and asked what was wanted. Being told he brought the saddlebags to the door, slung them over the fence and whirled suddenly back into the house.

I then went to Greencastle, and just as I had stabled my horse the town clock struck twelve. I then had near or quite a half a mile to walk to my boarding house, often thinking of the man who had caused me to be out so late.

    A demon drunk, and maddened fool,
    To what a hight would he arrive,

O'er angels, God and men would rule,
    And all as filthy from him drive.

The Indiana copperhead,
    He drove me from his home by night,
For I to him had something said,
    That did not suit a drunkard quite.

How like the devil he did look,
    In that to which he did pretend,
When he 'gainst Michael undertook
    For corpse of Moses to contend.

As Michael pure? Indeed not I,
    Nor ever thus myself could see;
Nor quite like his was my reply,
    Yet strictly true as words can be.

If true, the charge against him brought,
    And justly we him devilish call,
How humbling then must be the thought,
    The same is true against us all.

How gladly all to Christ should go,
    Their every sin and want confess,
Rejoicing much this truth to know,
    In him is life and righteousness,

But for a dying Savior's love,
    The Spirit's renovating grace,
We could not dwell with God above,
    And there in peace behold his face.

I would myself to Him submit,
    And in His sovereign grace confine,
Me for His service well to fit,
    And in the way of duty guide.

May He himself to me reveal,
    As from the shining seats above,
And make my inmost spirit feel,
    The strength of never dying love.

That hath all human knowledge passed,
    That gave the anxious spirits rest,
And all their fears far from them cast,
    With joy too full to be expressed.

How I could then for sinners pray,
    And show backsliders what they need,
And to transgressors teach the way,
    And anxious souls to Jesus lead.

155

> And all that I from God receive,
> As means of good through faith employ,
> That many sinners may believe,
> And have an endless life of joy.

In this land of plenty, often while participating at a well furnished table, I thought of my family and how differently they might be faring, and possibly suffering for some of the commonest comforts of life. But as my feeling were frequently and deeply harrowed in this way, I received a letter by two of my daughters at home, giving the comforting information that the family was well, and getting along as well as could be expected under existing circumstances. This news was so refreshing that for most one night—

> Sweet sleep, unmindful of her charge,
> Left thought to wander much at large.

Having obtained an outfit for the winter, on the 24th of November, facing a cold and violent wind, I left for Terrehaute, through which I passed the next day through a multitude of wagons loaded with wood and provisions for the soldiers' wives.

> While bright and starry, striped clouds,
> Were gayly floating in the air,
> Which seemed to say that all was right.
> The walks were lined with eager crowds,
> The cheering, welcome scene to share,
> With tokens true of great delight.

The following night I lodged in Clark county, Ill., with a good old Scotchman, who could afford to have a family altar illumined with a lamp for the feet and a light to the path in a home sanctuary.

> *From which the daily offerings rise,
> With rich perfume of odors sweet,
> Beyond the vail, above the skies,
> Before the throne and mercy seat.

> Where contrite hearts have access free,
> With such the Lord delights to meet,
> With sight restored gives them to see,
> The things that make their joy complete.

While at this house I read some in a book written by a

Rev. V, 8.

refugee from South Carolina. His description of things there corresponded so well with what I had witnessed in other places, that I thought it would be well for something of the kind to be put out by one from another part of the south, bearing witness to facts with regard to things there that should be known in the north. I thought that when I would get to the south part of the state, I would set in to prepare such a work; and hoped thereby to have access to the people, so as to affect more good than I could in any other way, for as things had been, my time appeared to be spent almost in vain, so far as affecting any moral good to others was concerned, which had been a source of disquietude to me during most of my time in the north.

Friday, the 27th being rainy and disagreeable, in the afternoon I inquired along the road for work, and found a man who gave me a job on a clock. In his countenance I read a good deal that did not afford a flattering prospect for a pleasant time, and his words and manners proved to be of a rough and disagreeable kind, and much qualified with profane language, the tasty finish of modern style; but by being dexterously evasive, and making every start of conversation toward an unwelcome subject, to be an occasion to be reminded of, and to introduce something interesting and amusing, I thereby succeeded in diverting and chasing the disagreeable and annoying subject of politics mostly out of sight, till I had the clock ready for trial and placed it on my knee. When the family were eagerly looking on and the clock commenced ticking, I gravely said :—

> Now it starts to tell the tale of woe,
> Time is passing, shortly you must go.

I thought this perhaps was a lucky hit, for I heard no more bad language that I recollect of from that man.

Whether this had anything to do with the matter or not, things passed smoothly on, and when the clock was finished and another was brought, which was not finished until the next morning, and when it was discharged another was brought forward. This suited the time very well, for the morning was snowy and very cold.

When the work was finished the landlord paid the charge like a gentleman, and appeared to feel an interest in giving me all the information he could with regard to the road.

I set out again through the wind and snow, over freezing mud and ice, and soon got into the prairie, where I could hardly keep warm walking in a double suit of clothes, and before night the ice would bear a horse, so that I progressed slowly; and late in the evening I learned that I would have to lodge with Germans, who were Roman Catholics, which was contrary to my wishes. After night I got to a place of lodging in Titopolis, where I remained over Sabbath and was kindly treated.

The house was well furnished with pictures of the Savior, his mother, saints and crosses, which to me was quite impressive. As they could not talk much English, I had a good opportunity for reading and reflection, without much interruption. I also attended church,—the first and only time I was ever in one of the kind, and thought it was wisely ordained, though contrary to my wishes, that I should stop at that place, where with my own eyes and ears I witnessed a confirmation of that which I had read, heard and seen representations of.

Though the day was so cold that water would freeze on a person's hair before he could walk ten steps, yet they had no fire in the church except the candles that were burning round the altar. And although I heard two discourses from one person in all, it was in an unknown tongue to me. I saw them applying holy water, and performing many signs and bodily exercises; facing about, bowing, kneeling, making the sign of the cross, and many such like things they did. I saw many pictures, images and representations of which I cannot now speak particularly. I beheld until I thought I was cold enough to leave, and did so, not knowing that the priests were going to take the sacrament that day, which I would willingly have witnessed for once.

When I returned from church the lady, who had remained at home, informed me that enduring the cold at church was a part of their religion; that the priests frequently went bareheaded in cold weather, and that some of the people occasionally walked barefoot to their graveyard and back before sunrise. I said they had relatives buried there, I supposed. She said, Yes. I understood it all as I had long ago been informed, with regard to such practices. While in this family, the remarkable contrast between the features and complexion of the oldest and the other children
—14

of the family, reminded me of some of Maria Monk's awful disclosures concerning the sanctification of brides by priests.

From this man (who, as I supposed, had his information and notions of political policy from the intelligent priests), I learned that they thought that a republican form of government would not do, and that they were not in favor of the northern and southern states being united under the old government. They also had the understanding that the French had no design to meddle with American affairs while they remained divided, but would not suffer them to be united if they could prevent it.

On the 7th of December I arrived at Parson Hamilton's, in the section of country where I had intended to winter. There I spent some time among acquaintances and working on clocks, and getting information with regard to wages and work of various kinds. Having improved much in health, and being tired of wandering continually from place to place, I made arrangements for boarding, bought food for wintering my horse, and went to cutting wood. I also made some arrangements for engaging in the present work.

I began chopping in large timber, but being out of practice I soon began to fail and had to quit the business. I then started out afoot, at my previous occupation, and on the last day of the old year I faced the snow storm in which I was caught some distance from my boarding, and began the new year wandering in the snow among the Jackson county hills, from which I began to make back toward my boarding place, in Union county, where I arrived in the night on Friday the 2d of January, 1864, and met with my son and nephew, who had come to spend the winter in that country.

The weather being severe and my health poor, perhaps from previous exposure, I spent most of my time within doors, with friends, sometimes working at my trade and sometimes reviewing English grammar, preparatory to commencing to write my intended work, but my health was such that I was unfit for much of anything.

On the 12th, having seated myself to begin my intended writing, the following letter was put into my hands, written by a nephew, at Camp Davis, January 4th, 1854:

"DEAR UNCLE:—I suppose you will be somewhat surprised to hear of me at this place. I came here on New

Year's day, and it will be one month to-night since I left home last. I started four times before I quite made the trip.

Our folks are enjoying good health at present. There has been a good deal of sickness since you left home, and a good many deaths. Last fall was a year ago, fever was in almost every family of the neighborhood, and, with few exceptions, death has taken one out of the families; though I suppose you have had news from home, before this time, by Mr. Wm. R——.

My father died early in the fall, and all the rest of the family were sick. We have all been afflicted by our Heavenly Father, yet not as much as we deserved. I have gone through many changes since I saw you last, yet all I ask is that I may receive grace to improve my greatest afflictions, and to be enabled to glorify my Heavenly Father, through all my race on earth.

I am at last separated from my home and friends, in a world of temptation and sin. As I said before, this is the fourth time I have tried to get away from the Confederacy. I last left home about a month ago, intending to go north and not join the army, but when I came here they would not let me go north, and it was left to my choice whether I would join the army or go back home; and after some consideration and twice being taken up by the provost, I concluded to join the cavalry, although it was much against my will; but I could not think of going back to be chased with dogs. I made a narrow escape from them, and rather than bait them again I will keep out of their way.

Cousin Byington came with me, as he is seventeen years old; for in Missisippi they are taking folks at seventeen. As he is not eighteen he has not voluntered, but he has not got any employment yet, and it is rather a bad place here for working, and it is possible he can stay here until he can get some advice from you. He would like to be with the rest of you, but it may be too cold there for him this winter. There was plenty of corn made in our neighborhood last year, and they are now very comfortably circumstanced.

Aunt Margaret requested me to tell you that she is doing very well, and is satisfied that you are out of the way of the Confederacy. I have some messages for the others of you from their friends at home. They would like to see you again, but do not wish you to be in as dangerous a place as the Confederacy.

As for going home, you need not think of that yet, unless you want to try the woods and dogs It is far worse than when you left home, but I cannot tell you everything now.

I wish I could see you all, and you don't know how glad I would be to be with my friends, for I have seen a good many people since I left home, and but two or three that were not profane.

I still remain your affectionate nephew,

W. J. F.

A response to this I had mailed the next day, and on the Sabbath following I preached in the neighborhood where my son and nephew were employed in Jackson county, There and at two other places, until the 17th of April, 1864, I preached at regular monthly appointments, for which I received no reward from men only my board when attending my appointments; though I was expected to do many deeds of charity for the widows, who were numerous in that country.

The following was received on the 28th of January, 1864:

CAMP DAVIS, Jan. 11, 1864.
1st Ala. Cav., Co. A.

——But to say something about home I suppose would be most interesting to you. Indeed, I might say a good deal that would interest you, if I had time, and was not bothered with people talking around me.

As I said before, the people are enjoying at present very good health, and there was plenty of corn raised last year to do them, if they can get to keep it; but if things keep on as they have been doing, it will be very uncertain about that. In Alabama they have threatened to burn all that belonged to those whose people had left Dixie; but it is probable that they only wish to scare the Union people, as they have often tried to do before.

A few weeks before I left home, the cavalry was searching for you all: they had their dogs and they searched in the barns and houses all about, but they did not go through all the neighborhood. I lay out in the woods myself, to keep out of their way. The people that I have been with since I left home, had become just about as wild as deer. When they heard dogs barking, they would listen as closely as if their lives were in great danger, and even when I was at home, I did get a little that way myself, and was ab sent from meeting several times on that account, as the cavalry had sometimes molested people at such places. They came to see me twice.

The people in our country have got to making spinning and weaving their chief employment. There can scarcely be anything bought at Columbus now.

It may be you have not heard of all the deaths that have taken place during the last year. I will give you their names, though I cannot recollect the time exactly, but will give them as they took place:

Cousin Wm. L. L., cousin N. A. Feemster, father, aunt P. R., cousin M. D. F., cousin B. F. Mrs. S. G., Mrs. M. And in several of the families, there was not one escaped being sick. Yet notwithstanding our afflictions seem to have been great, they were no doubt light in comparison with what we deserved, and it may be hoped that they were not without a good effect. And, added to all these, I am now separated from my home, and many of those whose company I delighted to have, and am placed in a world of sin and temptation; yet there is a friend who is both able and willing to protect those who put their trust in him. It is surely then my duty, as well as my privilege, to own him as my friend; and it is often surprising to me how little I feel inclined to love and trust in him. The army is rather an unsuitable place to be in. There does not appear to be any thought about religion; there is, indeed, some that appear more civil than others—and it is a place where one has not the opportunity of keeping the Sabbath as he would at home.

Cousin Jasper has been at home since last summer. He was taken prisoner at Vicksburg, and is paroled. He is toleraqly well now. Luther Love was at home when I left, though he may be taken up before this time, as they have got to taking persons from seventeen since I left home. I left about a month before Byington did.

But I must bring my letter to a close.

W. J. FEEMSTER.

As I had spent most of my wages for clothing, medicine, boarding and traveling, and did a good deal of work for which I received no pay, I found it necessary to keep at business in order to have some thing to go on; so that I had almost abandoned my purpose of writing altogether.

In my employment, I traveled over a considerable part of

Union, Jackson and Williamson counties, and back to the Mississippi river; but had to arrange my business so as to be in reach of my regular appointments. Much of the country was very rough and broken, abounding with lofty hills and deep ravines, huge rocks and frightful precipices; subterraneous caves, and coverts beneath projecting rocks, along rocky branches, hillsides and hollows, down which the waters rush and pour with rapid flow, and rattle, foam and roar among the rocks below. While in this region I had a call to the Bald Knob. Ascending this, I walked and lead my beast, and rested three times before we gained the top, from which to the south-west is to be seen the water in the Mississippi river, said to be ten miles distant. To the south, Jonesborough, and other places at a distance, are in plain view; and white houses and farms are seen on the distant hills to the east, beyond the railroad, and farms, and dwellings, and sugar camps scattered, and out of view along the hills and creeks between and far below. I had the understanding that many deserters had been harbored in this region. I had the spring before, seen the blue coats stationed at Jonesborough, and a citizen of South Pass, it w⌐as said, was killed by a deserter. This country, (Southern llinois) I understood bore the name of Egypt, and though there was a number of intelligent and worthy people in that country, I was surprised to find so many that could not read, and so many that could, who were so shamefully and criminally ignorant. If I was not mistaken—and I had a tolerably fair chance to know—these were generally what were called Copperheads, and were exceedingly mad against Lincoln, charging him with being the author of the war with all the consequent calamities, and with doing it to free the negroes, and that in violation of the constitution, &c.; while many of them did not know the difference between the constitution of the United States and the declaration of independence; and some did not know the difference between a score and a century Some could neither read, write, nor tell how to spell their own names; and though some of them could not furnish feed for a horse, nor a decent bed to sleep in, yet it was quite insulting to their superior dignity to think of being equalized with a negro.

I was not only annoyed, but often amused to see people so much like foolish beasts, scaring at their own tracks and shadows, and frightened at and running from a noise that proceeds from themselves.

On one occasion while I was employed in Williamson

county, (a place notorious for Copperheads and outrage) an old woman where I was at work, was full of distressing news concerning the war, drafting, the soldiers, negroes, &c. She had heard that the northern soldiers thought more of the negroes than they did of the whites, and a great many of them had taken black women back with them for wives. This, she appeared disposed to think might be true. A century being mentioned she asked what that was; and again, I think, asked if it was three-score.

Some of these southern counties abound with refugees, so that almost every old cabin, though not equal to a good stable, had people crowded into it to get out of the weather; and much was said against and disrespectfully of the refugees, and perhaps not without some good reason for it, and no doubt if they had all received their just recompense, some would have met the doom of the spy and the traitor. Though my opinion, founded upon evidence from observation, was, that those who talked most against them were not unfriendly to this class, the true reason of their disrespect being, that refugees, generally, were in for supporting the government, and were rapidly increasing the vote in that way, I so often heard them spoken of as a lazy, poor, heartless set of people, that I sometimes would make some apology for them, in view of their unfavorable and disheartening circumstances.

I had been so long and so much annoyed with contemptible theories, frivolous proofs and pretexts for absurd doctrine and unjustifiable practices, that I had taken to practicing a sort of retaliation for my own amusement. As tobacco affords pleasure to the acquired taste, so, there are other like things by a long association with which, we can some time derive pleasure from that which is contrary to our nature.

> Has Copperhads become so strong,
>   Through all Egyptian wilds so soon;
> So much have sung the negro song,
>   That every snake has learned the tune?
> For which they can refrain from sleep.
>   It gives to them so much delight,
> As into secret dens they creep,
>   Where late is heard the song at night.

On a certain night, after a lady had said the refugees were doing no good, for themselves, said I, "perhaps they are like hogs. You know that in a plentiful year, when they are in good order, and can find plenty to subsist upon, they are lively and in industrious, and are up and stirring early But when a scarce time comes, and they get poor and weak, they loose heart, give up, and lie about making little or no effort to obtain anything. Such may be the case with the refugees, who, having lost everything, have no heart to try to make anything more. Some who were present said they thought such a fortune would have that effect upon them.

Next morning, the old lady spoke against the refugees again, and when she had said a good deal for their discredit, said I, "I suppose I may take this all to myself, for I am a refugee?" She made the apology that she did not intend what she had said for all.

She then changed the subject to that of the insufferable wrong of making the negro equal with the white people. This had become a favorite subject with me for the mortification of foolish pride, though I had no occasion to introduce it myself, but sometimes, when introduced by others, was almost impolitely fond of it. I remarked that it appeared quite natural to us all to think and feel that we were better than a negro, but it was not so easy a matter to prove that it was so. She at first did not appear to think it hard to prove that they were an inferior and degraded race, and asked why it was that they were black? I said that was one thing we had never been told. He who made of one blood all nations to dwell upon the earth, saw fit to make different colors, but had not told us why, and if he esteemed one color above, or as preferable to, another, he had not told us which it was. How, then, could we find it out. She said black was a degraded color. I said we did not generally think so, but commonly were very fond of a nice suit of clothes, and expected then she would like to have a nice black dress, and would feel quite saucy. She (apparently losing sight of the subject) readily agreed that she would. Then, said I, the negro has the advantage, and is that much our superior. He has, by nature, what we have to get by art, and are proud to own as an artificial ornament. She then saw that she had beaten herself.

Some denied that a negro had a soul; others contended that they were an inferior race, and were made to be servants for white people, and that they were better off in that condition than they would be in any other. Some who could not read, said they had heard it read in the Old Testament that Cain had a mark put upon him, and they thought that was the color of the negro; for it was said that his seed should be servants upon servants, and they would bet me a treat that what they had said was in the old Bible somewhere.

I some times amused myself by asking some of those who had so much contempt for the thick liped, flat nosed, woolly headed negro, to tell wherein they were beetter than a negro. (They could not deny that many of them were more stout and active than most of the white people, could do as much or more work; many showed as much aptness and ingenuity to learn when they had an equal chance as the whites.) This they could not easily do, yet it would have been quite an insulting and ungentlemanly thing to have told them that they were no better than a negro, though some of them had no more education or intelligence, nor any better morals, nor even as good, as a majority of negroes in America. Yet they could not bear to be put on an equality with the negro; from which it would appear that they were no friends to progress and improvement; for to place them upon an average equality with American negroes, would raise them considerably in the scale of refinement, for a vast number of negroes are greatly their superiors in everything except features and color; and some in bondage and called negroes would excel them in these.

I was often shocked and distressed to see the degree of impudence, profanity and wickedness that prevailed among children or boys. On one occasion, in particular, at Anna Station, I saw a company of boys employed in exhibiting a scene, as I thought, of worse conduct than I had ever witnessed among as many of the most degraded negroes, that I had ever seen in the south, who had received the impress of the iron furnace of southern oppression. Surely, the parents of such offspring are guilty of preparing the earth for a curse, and are sowing the seeds of calamity and destruction to the country.

Children left to themselves, are taught to profane the Sabbath, using profane language, speaking evil of dignitaries, despising government, &c., were so prevalent that they cast a fearful gloom over the prospect of the future. So common were such things that when I fell in at a house of good morals and good family government, it was like the pleasant calm after a storm, and a little *paradise* in a wilderness of woe. These things are not confined to Egypt,

I continued in that country until after the middle of April. My son and nephew previous to this had gone back to Macon county, and I was tired of my wandering manner of living, and having heard that good wages were given on the praries, for farming as I thought probably I was able to follow that business, I resolved to go north and do so, if I could be suited.

About the 13th of April I wrote the Egpytian Son at the house of Parson Hamilton, where I spent many a pleasant season in the good old religious way, which I still remember with satisfaction. On the 17th I preached at two houses my last sermons in Egpyt; and on the 19th, started north, after having labored in that region from the 5th of December to that time.

It was always a satisfaction to me to fall in with people who appeared to be religious and true to the government: but sometimes I fared worse with them than with those who made no particular pretensions to either. For example: On my way north, I lodged with a man not far from Mount Vernon, who made tall pretensions to respect for the present administration, and made quite a show of religion in his family. He, as did the shipmen with Jonah, asked me with regard to whence I came, my country, people, &c., and professed great sympathy for people in my condition.

Next morning, as it was rainy, and I saw two dumb clocks in the house, I said it looked like I had stopped at the right place, as I did not wish to travel in the rain, and it looked like the clocks needed something done for them, and repairing clocks was my occupation. He said if I could do it he would like to have me put one in order. I went at it and found a job that kept me till about noon, and when it was finished another was presented for repair, and when it was done a third was brought, and when it was through with, the day was nearly spent and I remained till next morning. I ate no dinner, and my horse was unwell and did not eat much. When about to leave I asked how matters stood between us? He said, that was for me to say, in part; and asked what I was going to charge him. I felt a little at a loss to know what would be right. He said his charge was three dollars. I said I supposed he professed to be a scripture abiding man, and if he wanted to do as he would wish to be done by, I would try to be satisfied. He gave me his hand, as I understood, in token that we were even. At the prices then, what I had done would not have been less than four dollars.

As I went on toward Salem, where I expected to attend church on Sabbath. I stopped at a house to get out of the rain, when I fell in with a book agent, who was soliciting orders for Dr. Gunn's Home Book of Health. As he lived at Salem, and it was an unfavorable time for canvassing, he started to accompany me to that place. But we were detained by high water till Monday. In the meantime he used his influence to get me to buy a book and to become an agent, representing it as a business at which I could do well.

After some reflection upon the subject, I thought that occupation, in connection with the one I had, might enable me to get along better. I had some doubts of my ability to do well on a farm. It was getting late in the season, and people had generally got their engagements made for farming. But I went on to Kinmundy, intending if not better suited in business about there, to return and take an agency. I remained in that section of country about two weeks, during which I wrote some poems; some at the suggestion of some of my fellow refugees from Alabama, who, like myself, had left wife and children in a far distant land.

I again returned to Salem, and after making the necessary arrangements for canvassing for Gunn's work in Edgar county, with the privilege of following my previous occupation, when to my interest to do so.

I went to the allotted field of operation in Kansas township, where, after getting my horse on pasture, on the 24th of May I pursued my occupation under unfavorable and discouraging circumstances. People were much divided on politics, and were full of jealousy and unkind feeling toward one another, and were calling each other abolitionists and Lincoln hirelings: copperheads, butternuts and traitors. There had been a riot at Charleston, on the west, and at Paris, on the east, and each party had their own story about the matter, which cast the blame on their opposers, and many threats were making, and fears were entertained by many of serious outrage and violence; and if I was capable of judging correctly some went to extremes on both sides, and indulged in unjustifiable speeches and charges against others for that of which they were not guilty, though there were some on both sides who were little better than the worst charges called for; for there were some on both sides who were no honor to any civil society or good cause; and while each were criminating, and laying the blame of all our troubles and calamities on the othe,r to my sorrow the honest conviction of my own mind was, that many, if not the majority, of both parties, were acting the part of deadly foes to the country. Because the love of God is not in them, His fear is not before their eyes; He is not in their thoughts, the way of peace (with Him) they have not known. They desire not the knowledge of His ways, (if not in their hearts, by their actions.) They have said, "What is the Lord that we should fear Him? Who is the Almighty, that we should obey Him?" They have spoken perverse things. Too many have done abominable wickedness. They set their mouth against heaven, and their tongue walketh through 'the earth. The show of their countenance witnesseth against them. They declare their sin as Sodom; they hide it not. Woe unto them, for they have gone in the way of Cain, and run greedily after the error of Balaam for reward. Many despise government; presumptuous are they, self-willed, not afraid to speak evil of dignities, and of things they understand not; many of whom perish in their own corruption. Many have hearts exercised with covetous practices. Some grind the face of the poor, oppress the fatherless and widow, and mistreat the stranger. Cursed children, who have forsaken the right way, going astray from the old way, wandering in forbidden paths according to the course of this world; lead captive by the wicked one at his will, under the influence of the prince of the power of the air, the spirit that now rules in the hearts of the children of disobedience, and leads to the practice of that on account of which the wrath and judgments of God cometh upon them. How the precious of the earth, comparable with fine gold, are mixed with the vile. The fine gold had become dim; the silver dross, and the wine mixed with water; and, instead of humility, meekness and lowliness of heart and contrition of spirit, is impenitence, haughtiness and spiritual wickedness in high places, and much devotion to the lust of the flesh, the lust of the eye and the pride of life.

And those characters abound in consequence of which we are told that perilous times are to be in the latter days, a descriptive catalogue of which is given in the III of 2 Tim., whose moral influence is like the malignant blast, and rank with the pestilential effluvium of putrefaction, disease and death swept from the sepulchral shades.

I was watched with a suspicious eye by both parties; sometimes treated kindly and sometimes with coldness and indifference by both: and sometimes rudely and contemptibly, having reproachful insinuations cast upon me. I met with some called copperheads, who treated me in the kindest and most generous manner, and so of those called abolitionists.

About the 25th of June I wrote for about as many books as I expected to receive orders for by the 1st of July, but wheat harvest coming on, I could get but few more orders; and, as hands were wanted in harvest, I went at that, but was not able for the business, but quit and repaired on clocks till the books came on. As I was a stranger, and it was a time of deception and suspicion, when people were deceiving and being deceived, I could get no means of distributing but on foot and horseback. This was a hard way for a weakly man to make his was through the world.

In this way I delivered to subscribers in two townships, and before I got through, riding, exposed to the sun, had so injured my health, that I had to rest part of the day, to be able to travel the remainder. Owing to failures on the part of subscribers, I had a considerable lot of books left on hands, and had to apply for new territory to canvass in.

It was now the middle of July, and people were still busy with their wheat and hay, and it was an unfavorable time for canvassing. I was in poor health and much dissatisfied with the way my life was passing, and determined that when the books were disposed of, I would write a pamphlet, which I thought would be done in a few weeks, and then I would travel, lecture and distribute; and perhaps in that way I might affect some good in the world, and I again went to work on clocks, and to get subscribers in Embarrass and Buck townships for my unsold books. There I was sometimes working at clocks, sometimes getting subscriptions, and sometimes visiting till the first week in September, and still had not obtained subscribers for all the books.

On the 15th of September, after delivering the books subscribed for, I commenced the long contemplated work.

CHAPTER X.

INCIDENTS OE TRAVEL IN GRANDVIEW, KANSAS AND BUCK TOWNSHIPS—SOME OF THE CONCOMITANTS OF MY SOJOURN IN EDGAR.

During my travels in Grand View and Kansas I was twice invited or ordered to go out of people's houses. Twice in one neighborhood, I received very abusive language from persons who were perhaps twenty or thirty years my juniors. Each threatened me with a dreadful beating, and exhibited their fists. One cursed shamefully: both called me an *old liar*. They could say all manner of evil against me, but I must say nothing against them. No! not the truth. With them brute force was preferable to logic for the decision of moral differences.

> Now by what rule do such proceed?
>   First inward force the rugged gag,
>   And then accuse, condemn and brag,
> When none can dare oppose the deed.
>
> Though copper called and abolish,
> They both, I thought, were lamperfish;
> Nor dove nor lamb could in them find,
> But much, I thought, of serpent kind.
> Now do you ask what is each name?
> I here can tell what is the same:
> That of a coat made for a chill,
> And of a man who keeps a mill.
> *They gave the martyr's name to one,
> †The other Jacob's youngest son.
> How well they use their mortal tongue!
> Their acts, how manly, noble, brave,

---

*S. Mille, †B. Chilcote.

171

> For men so healthy, stout and young,
> With one then blooming for the grave.
> They little think in all their boast,
> Presumptuous, vain and self conceit,
> They soon to death must yield the ghost,
> And all their deeds in judgment meet,
> Their crimes of every time and place,
> All rise and stare them in the face.

Not many miles from the residence of these men, I once attended meeting among a class of people who appeared to have a great dread of negro equality, but I had no recollection of ever having witnessed half as much shamefully bad conduct in a congregation of southern negroes; for they knew how, and did behave themselves with much more decency and civility; and to equalize these people with those negroes in this respect, would elevate them to a much more respectable and worthy degree of decency and refinement of manners. And, if I was not mistaken, I had seen negroes who could far excel their speaker in a discouse. In that country, I thought many ought to be pitied for their ignorance, and punished for their vices, for they appeared to despise good order and government; were self-willed and presumptuous, speaking evil of rulers and of things which they did not understand; calling the soldiers abolitionists, Lincoln hirelings and hell hounds, and were also threatening to resist the government, but when drafted, took to the brush like rabbits.

> In dark retreats they shunned the light,
> As doleful beasts and owls of night,
> In nearer wild where vagrants roam,
> Obtained a mild Canada home.

While I was in Buck township, being confined most of one day with fever and flux, at night after the fever had left me and I was sitting up a while, the landlord and a young man working with him, had a curiosity to know where I was from, and why I had left the south, and appeared astonishingly green with regard to the true state of things in that country, and the causes of it; and were clamoring against the northern administration.

The young man talked in a very excitable manner, with as much fury and acrimony as I ever witnessed in the south among the most rabid secesh. He sentenced Lincoln and his allies to certain perdition and said more hard things of the government than I could recollect in many days. He said we had no liberty of speech any more; that Lincoln had violated the constitution, and trampled upon the rights of the people, and if any one said anything against the hellish policy, he was jerked up and put in prison, and tried contrary to the constitution; and there was not a worse despotism on the top of the globe! Lincoln had assumed more power than the crowned heads of Europe dare to do; and if the draft that was then talked of took place, there would be no election for President at all, but Lincoln would proclaim himself Emperor of the United States; and many such like things he said. If I do not give his language verbatim, I give the sense conveyed to me, in his own words, as well as I can recollect.

He went on to state that Lincoln had kicked the southern states out of the Union, and then had gone to murdering and plundering them, and stealing their negroes. He assumed that it was all done for the sake of the negroes. I told him he could not impose such stuff upon me, for I knew better. I knew that the leaders in the south were making arrangements for seceding, and had intentionally contrived matters so as to get a pretext for seceding, and they got the excuse they wanted; and some of them boasted of having accomplished their object for a separation of the Union. And I knew that before Lincoln had anything to do with the government, and before the presidential election, calls were made and some volunteers were obtained, professedly for the purpose of going to prevent Lincoln from taking his seat at Washington, if elected.

He said he did not like to dispute a man's word, but he would give me to understand that he did not think that was so, and asked something with regard to some other matters. I told him it appeared to be time for me to keep my mouth shut, for he had as much as told me that I lied, and I did not take much interest in conversation under such circumstances. He said he did not aim to dispute my word. He supposed I thought it was so, but *he* had seen nothing of the kind in public print. I said there was no getting around it. as I had stated it as something that I knew, it was either a truth or a known, wilful falsehood, and nothing else could be made of it.

But he kept on talking, and undertook to prove from the

Bible that slavery is right; and censured and abused the government for meddling with the negroes. I made some remarks with regard to some rules in the Bible that he would do well to notice.

He replied in an overbearing manner, "I know as well what's in the Bible as you do," and went on with his hideous, brutish talk; and, speaking of Lincoln and his allies, said hell was sure of all such men.

I asked him if he was sure he was not on the way there himself, and told him he did not follow the advice of Solomon, nor the example of Elihu of old; and, *well* as he was acquainted with the Bible, it was easy to see that he did not know what was referred to; but, as he was so knowing, he needed no explanation. I remarked that if everybody that had talked against Lincoln was taken up for it, a great many more would be taken up than had been, and the prisons would be crowded with such people; and I said I sometimes felt that I would be glad that the people who were complaining of hard times and no liberties in the country, had to try it a while under the southern government; for if they were to take the same liberty there that they were doing here, they would soon be put where they would make no more noise; for though I had never taken the liberty to say half the hard things against that government that they had against this, I had been threatened with a rope; and, said I: "Though I claim to have as much and more reason to say evil things of the leaders of the south than you have against those here, yet no one has ever heard me make use of such language as you have been doing. If I had done so I would have been nothing the better for it. Such a course is only calculated to increase bad feelings, and to produce a worse state of things. If others have done wrong, reproaching and reviling make their past actions neither better nor worse, nor alters the case; though it may provoke many to do worse than they would otherwise be disposed to do. And while we are all looking at, magnifying, quarrelling about and condemning the faults of others, and justifying ourselves, and indulging and glorying in our own faults, we have no reason to hope for much good to come to us.

He said many innocent people had been taken up here and refused a lawful trial, &c. I said I knew nothing of those cases, but if he did, it was not my place to dispute and contradict the truth of it.

*—15

When he had calmed down and retired, I asked his age, and learned that he was quite young to be so exceeding wise. Copperhead and all, the landlord treated me quite hospitably, for which I owe him a debt of gratitude and good will.

   And hope that by another spring,
   He'll leave the slough and be a king ;
   And when this happy change he makes,
   Will help to crush the poison snakes.
   Though evils do from mires flow,
   Good fruits abundant there may grow.

News from the south, through a correspondent in southern Illinois, with dates of times when written and when received:

        ANNA, Ill., July 20, 1864.

MR. FEEMSTER :—Wm. J—— is just in from Dixie. He said that T—— M—— was going to start north in a few days; his wife was sick, or he would have come with the crowd that started in June. Your family are anxious to hear from you. He said your family was all well, as far as he knew; and if they were not, he thinks some of the boys would have said something about it as they were passing; and T—— M—— had just been down to your house.
    Yours,   J. F. T.

This was received the first of August.

        ANNA, Ill., Aug. 22, 1864.

DEAR SIR :—Yours of —— came to hand in due time. We are all well. W—— R—— is at Centralia; his brother F—— is on board the United States ship of war Susquehana. He was captured in Georgia and volunteered in the navy. J—— C—— is here from Fayette; he left on the 18th of July. He says the rebs have killed all of our friends. They shot T. M. and his son H. They hung his wife till she told where he was. They made him go to old man J. R's, and they burnt his house and hung him. They went to M. R's, big B. P's, A. T's, H. P's, W. G's, P, M's and W. M's, and several others, and hung them all on Sunday, the 17th of July. Some of them were hanging late on Monday evening when C. left the settlement.

I have received news from J—— M——, at Decatur, Ala., confirming the above.
This was received on the 3d of September, 1864. The names were in full, where I give initials only.

ANNA, Ill., Sept. 25, 1864.

——D. J. G's family is here, just from Dixie. They say T. M. is not dead. They say the cavalry hung old man J. R., Mr. R. and W. P. They burned some houses. Mrs. G. saw the limb on which they were hung. They burnt the old man J. R's house and immodestly mutilated him before they hung him, and gave orders that if any buried him they should be hung. They did this murder on the 17th of July, being Sunday, and the old man hung on a walnut tree at his gate, till Tuesday night, when M. D. went by night and dug a hole in his garden and buried him, after the buzzards had pulled out both his eyes. M. R's daughters cut him down and buried him, and Penington's family buried him.

Sir, this is a true statement of the case, as Mrs. G. and Mrs. R., M. Tucker and several others, have seen their graves and the families. They took T. Mallory, and several others, to Tuscaloosa. They first reported that they had hung them, but these women say they have not.

There desperadoes were legally commissioned. Captain Wm. Godlden was in command of the squad, and had thirty men. Drake was lieutenant; Col. Headen was in command, with his headquarters at Fayette Court House. They were murdered for their loyalty.

Your family are doing as well as could be expected. They are making straw hats. Those women say they heard no complaint from them, and if there was anything wrong they think they would have heard it. B. F. T.

Received September 29, 1864.

On the 29th of October I received a few lines from my son, mailed Memphis, Tenn., from which I understood that he was a soldier, as I suppposed, drafted. This added another to the troubles and sources of care and anxiety in life. But I cherished the hope that it might be with me, as with Jacob of old, when he had to give up Benjamin, though, he said, all these things go against me, yet it was all for the best for him and his family. The latest from my son was dated January 1st, '65. He was about leaving Memphis for New Orleans.

CHAPTER XI

CAUSE, CURE AND PREVENTIVE OF DIVISION, WAR AND CALAMITY.

In my travels I have met with many people and things, I think, worthy of my respect and high esteem, which have been sources of comfort and encouragement to me. I also think I have seen a great deal of the reverse, which has been a source of trouble, disappointment and discouragement, which spread a dark vail over the future, and filled the mind with painful apprehensions of what is yet to come. For the premonitions of Divine displeasure are not few. In some sections of country many are complainers, murmurers, with whom nothing in the natural, political or religious world appeared to be right. They find fault with the seasons, the rulers, the preachers, professors, and other people. "Can prove all creeds and actions wrong but their own; their own most wrong."

I have had occasion to remark that if one like Moses was set at the head of government, and acted according to the direction of God in all that he did, it would not please all the people; but some would think he ought to be killed. Or if a man had the control of the weather, and caused it to be just as it is: in perfect accordance with the Divine will and direction, they would think he ought not to live; and of course if the works and ways of a perfectly holy, just and good Being cannot please the people, nothing that is just and right will. And it is not to be wondered at, if they are opposed to, and speak evil of good things and good people.

I have sometimes prevented disagreeable, and, to me, unwelcome conversation, by remarking that we are all Adam's children, and manifest the same disposition that we did when first called to an account for his disobedience. We are disposed to lay the blame of our calamities upon others when our own sins are the procuring cause. He said, "That woman!" I have endeavored to lead persons to the consideration of the vanity and unprofitableness of spending our time quarrelling about the wrong doings of others that we cannot alter nor prevent; while we neglect to correct those of our own, and of those whom it is our duty to control, and by which we might do more good for ourselves and others than we could in any other way.

The look and actions of some with whom I met, reminded me of some spoken of old, who were possessed of devils. Their language and disposition indicated some fearful derangement within. They were sharp to detect fault, and fierce in their accusations against others, while themselves were the servants of sin; acting as if they thought they had license to indulge in the greatest crimes, without dishonor to themselves. A rough, irreverent and immoral manner of speech too generally prevails in most places I have visited. In too great a portion of our country, family government is, to a great extent, a practically insignificant thing. Children are growing up without proper restraint and control, trained to habitual disobedience to parents, self-willed, presumptuous, despisers of government, impatient of restraint, to be evil speakers and inventors of evil things, fit instruments to corrupt, overturn and destroy national government. Or as natural brute beasts, to be taken and destroyed themselves. Covetousness, falsehood, deception, fraud, oppression, contempt of holy things, and forgetfulness of God, have been too prevalent, both north and south. They have trampled upon His precepts, thrown down His altars, perverted judgment, profaned His Sabbaths, made His house a den of thieves. They have hated reproof, refused instruction, despised His counsel, hated knowledge, rejected His offers, slighted His invitations, disobeyed His commands, closed their eyes, stopped their ears, stiffened their necks, hardened their hearts, not desiring the knowledge of His ways.

In consequence of these things the wrath of God has come upon the children of disobedience; and not peace and harmony, but division and the sword have been sent upon the people of America, who have become a sinful nation, a people laden with iniquity, who have forgotten the Lord and He also has forgotten their children, and has given them over to the sword. Hell has enlarged itself without measure, and multitudes are descending into it. "He that being often reproved hardeneth his neck, shall be suddenly destroyed, and that without remedy."

Many were often reproved, and faithfully warned of that which should come as a snare upon the whole earth; but, seeing, they did not perceive, and hearing, they did not understand, till that which is written has come upon them. Behold ye despisers and wonder and perish.

It was necessary that the loftiness of man should be humbled, and that the haughtiness of men should be brought low. And because the daughters of Zion were haughty, instead of their splendid mansions, profusion of delicacies, ornament, perfume and gaudy attire, this prophecy has been fulfilled upon some of them. "Thy men shall fall by the sword, and the mighty in the war; and her gates shall lament and mourn; and she, being desolate, shall sit upon the ground." Isa. III, 25, 26.

Here we have the primary cause of all our calamities. "Is there no balm in Gilead? is there no physician there? Why, then, is not the health of the daughter of my people recovered?" Jer. VIII, 22. "Because they are all estranged from me through their idols." Eze. XIV, 6. "Ye have said it is vain to serve God, and what profit is it that we have kept his ordinance, and that we have walked mournfully before the Lord of hosts? and now we call the proud happy; yea, they that work wickedness are set up; yea, they that tempt God are even delivered." Mal. III. "I also will choose their delusions, and will bring their fears upon them. I will number you to the sword, and ye shall bow down to the slaughter; because when I called ye did not answer; when I spoke ye did not hear; but did evil before mine eyes, and did those things wherein I delighted not." Isa. LXV, 12, and LXVI, 4. "Hast thou not procured this unto thyself, in that thou hast forsaken the Lord thy God, when He led thee by the way? Thine own wickedness shall correct thee, and thy backslidings shall reprove thee. Know, therefore, and see that it is an evil thing and bit*er, that thou hast forsaken the Lord thy God, and that my fear is not in thee." Jer. II, 16, 19. "What shall we do, then?" Luke III, 10. "Return unto me, and I will return unto you, saith the Lord." Mal. III, 7 "Yea, let them turn every one from his evil way, and from the violence that is in their hands." Jonah, III, 8. "If ye be willing and obedient, ye shall eat the good of the land; but if ye refuse and rebel ye shall be devoured, for the mouth of the Lord hath spoken it." Isa. I, 19, 20.

Here the remedy is set before us, and the manner of using it. "Let us search and try our way, and turn again to the Lord." Lam. III, 40. "Come, let us return unto the Lord, for He hath torn and He will heal us; He hath smitten and He will bind us up." Hos. VI, 1. He will be as a lamp to our feet and a light to our path.

How completely is the way marked out for our safe return to peace and prosperity, and by which we may inherit the promise to the obedient. "Why art thou cast down, O my soul? and why art thou disquieted within me? Hope thou in God, for I shall yet praise him for the help of his countenance." Psa. XLI, 5, 11. "If a man's ways please the Lord, he maketh even his enemies to be at peace with him." Solomon.

How important that we attend to that counsel, which, like the harbinger of Christ in the spirit and power of Elias, would turn the hearts of the fathers to the children, and the hearts of the children to the fathers, and the disobedient to the wisdom of the just, to make ready a people prepared for the Lord." Mal IV, 6, Luke I, 17.

When this is effected so as to lead the people to observe the moral and civil law, given to the chosen people of old, and to teach and enforce them with the some diligence and strictness with which they were then required to do it, which is the same thing that St. Paul calls "the nurture and admonition of the Lord," this would secure the peace prosperity and happiness of our nation. Though the typical law, which was a shadow of the good things to come, has been fulfilled, and the shadow has ended in the substance, and the true light has come, yet the precepts of the moral law, and the principles inculcated in the laws for the civil government of ancient Israel, are just as necessary for the maintenance of good order and the best interests of society now, as they were then. As they were better calculated to accomplish this object than anything that human wisdom could devise, so they are now. The greatest calamities they suffered then were in consequence of departing from those principles, and so they are yet. A conformity to those laws secured prosperity and happiness then, and so it would now. Whatever system of government is the most efficient in preventing evil, and promoting the peace and happiness of society, is the best government. Who that is acquainted with human nature does not know that if the old law had been executed in our country, even to putting the ungovernable son, the Sabbath breaker, blasphemer and murderer to death, and to the exaction of an eye for an eye and a tooth for a tooth, that the amount of damage, suffering and loss of life from crime, and the execution of criminals would not have been one-tenth part of what it has been, as matters have been conducted.

As it is the same unchangeable God, who is the Judge of all the earth and will do right, who still takes cognizance of the nations of the earth, and the relations his creatures sustain to him and to each other, are the same. The duties they owe to Him and to one another, are the same. In the nature of things, their comfort and welfare are as much dependent upon the performance of those duties. They are under as strong obligations to observe the rules best calculated to secure the performance of those duties; and a nation will be happy and prosperous in proportion as they do, or do not those duties.

From the XXVIIth to the XXXIVth chapter of Deut. are set forth the curses, distresses and woful afflictions and calamities for disobedience, and the blessings, comforts and encouragement for obedience. In their obedience they were to be blessed in their family, person and property, and in all that they put their hand to; but, in case of disobedience, they were to be cursed in all these things.

By performing and complying with the conditions upon which temporal and spiritual blessings were offered, they enjoyed both. Faith in the Messiah secured spiritual life, and obedience, which is its legitimate fruit, secured prosperity, a crown of glory and an inheritance, and a promise to their children. The same cause will secure the same results still. We have the Bible full of instruction suited to our case, to which if we attend, all will be healed in due time. We will seek first the kingdom of God and his righteousness, and such things as are for our good will be added unto us. If we know these things happy are we, if we do them; but if we will not, then behold we have sinned, and be assured our sins will find us out, and the way of peace we shall not know, but destruction and misery are in our way. The earth will disclose their blood and no more cover the slain, and their "blood shall be upon us and our children." "That which brings forth briars and thorns is nigh unto cursing, whose end is to be burned."

THE EGYPTIAN SONG

WRITTEN ABOUT THE TIME OF MY DEPARTURE FROM SOUTHERN ILLINOIS.

On Egypt's rugged hills I stand,
And think of Dixie's ruined land,
The happy scenes that come to mind,
Their anxious eyes no more can find.

They for the Lord too little care,
And he no longer hears their prayer;
They have too long abused his grace,
And now from them he hides his face.

He has an ear for those that crave,
And mighty is his arm to save;
'Gainst him their crimes have been so great,
They from his mercy separate.

Sodom's and Egypt's crimes they know,
This fact their features plainly show,
In those black crimes which they have wrought,
They still persist and hide them not.

By Egypt's plagues and Sodom's woe,
They should have learned their doom to know,
And by those omens understand
What still awaits their guilty land.

Whence here to Egypt many fly,
And mourn and sicken, droop and die,
Egyptian darkness here they feel,
Of negroes hear peal upon peal,

Here copperheads are thick as fleas,
Say copperheads and whisky bees,
Yea, butternuts, and such as these,
Are full of spite at refugees.

They wish the negroes dead indeed,
Much rather than to have them freed;
Would rather have the land destroyed,
Than negroes in the war employed.

At Abe they curse, and rage, and grin,
As throbs a traitor's heart within;
They love for Davis much to say,
For him to save us lie and pray.

Their solemn oaths they freely break,
As they the Union ranks forsake,
And back to Egypt's hills they come,
To hide in holes away from home.

The friends of those that run away,
How oft we hear them falsely say:
"The woes that on the nation fall—
'T was Lincoln's war that caused them all."

And, to make the charge look bigger,
Say he did it for the nigger;
For this is all they ever see:—
'T was done to set the negro free.

If black and white are equal made,
The land in ruins must be laid;
As for their life they cannot see,
How justice makes a negro free.

Though they do murder swear and curse,
Of demons none were ever worse;
To them it still is clear as day,
No negro can be good as they.

And now, to cap and crown the whole,
Some say a negro has no soul.
At this a Foundland dog might laugh—
One with a soul and one with half!

Has not an ass got wit to see,
What a mulatto's part must be ?
But be it wicked or unwise,
They oft are sold as merchandise.

In high places many figure,
By the sale of mule and nigger ;
The funds of others much increase,
With price of brother, son and neice.

The white is best, who dare disptue?
The black has been his prostitute ;
And sure, here is a sign of good :
They those can sell who show their blood.

With these they make a bright display,
For half-souled negroes all are they.
How great the white, it can't be said,
So thinks the bright, the copperhead.

And after all we here unfold,
One thousandth part has not been told;
Though "Satan trembles when he sees"
A righteous negro on his knees—

The copperhead can hard remain,
And of the waste of time complain.
Would you their inward temper know ?
There is a way that truth to show :

They are as demon's, raging mad.
If one with truth is heard to say :
A negro—though not half so bad,—
Is equally as good as they,

Their wicked actions on them tell,
That they are heirs of death and hell
How sick'ning then the sight to see,
How very good they claim to be?

Behold how lofty is their aim!
To more than saint they make a claim.
To many of the negro race
The Lord extends his saving grace.

The bread that down from heaven came,
To endless life gives them a claim,
To them he gives release from sin,
A heart renewed to dwell within.

And by their works they oft record
The grace of their redeeming Lord,
When in the dust their bodies lie,
Their souls shall rise above the sky.

The battle fought, the victory won,
They shine in glory as the sun.
Some this presume to their own shame,
They are their Maker's highest aim.

Pretense like these those whites have made,
They are of men the highest grade,
And have it so they surely will,
On them he lavished all his skill.

But they themselves too little know,
This truth their actions plainly show,
The depth of guile that in them lies,
Is little seen with blinded eyes.

As they the Lord did not obey,
He never cleansed their sins away.
How dreadful then will be their woe,
When what they are they truly know.

The place they occupy in hell,
How God approves will truly tell,
When as they are themselves they view,
Amid a lost and wailing crew.

With devils damned and negroes base,
And all the vile of Adam's race,
Will not they say to all who see,
Oh! clear the way for wretched me?

Give way ye base and let me low,
For I am worse than you I know;
Oh! guide me to the darkest place,
And hide me from the Judge's face.

May my abode there always be,
Where I his glory cannot see;
Might rocks and mountains on me fall,
So I could not be found at all.

Oh! awful state of deep despair,
Where hosts of wretched spirits are;
Who much beguiled by self-esteem,
Had such a wild and foolish dream,

They saw a merit on the skin,
But little thought of worth within;
Thus in their hue they saw a worth,
Which never grew from gracious birth.

Their hue they thought gave state so high
All grace hath wrought no such can buy;
Then let the living warning take,
And proper preparations make,

Before their days of mercy close,
And they be doomed to ceaseless woes;
Nor let them lose a moment's time,
Nor make excuse for any crime.

Nor ever boast of hue or race,
But trust alone to sovereign grace,
For this can end all foolish strife,
To every color give new life.

Yes, this can stop all wicked claims,
And fill the soul with righteous aims,
Which leads of evil to repent,
And makes with right to be content.

Which all to peace and comfort tend,
And bring about a happy end.
Now let us all this course pursue,
And grace will guide us safely through

A REFUGEE'S PARODY.

On Egypt's lofty hills I stand,
   And cast a thoughtful eye,
To Dixie's drear and wretched land,
   Whence friends of Union fly.

Oh! the unbroken, cruel scene,
   That rises to my sight,
There rabid rebs from country glean
   The men for them to fight.

There men as beasts where mercy fails,
   To scenes of carnage go,
And rocks and hills, and brooks and vales,
   With blood and murder flow.

Through all those wide and bloody plains,
   Shines one infernal ray,
Where Jefferson the rebel reigns,
   And drives all peace away.

No healing wind or peaceful breath,
   Can reach this blighted shore,
Wickedness, terror, pain and death,
   Prevail the kingdom o'er.

When I shall reach that captured place,
   With friends and kindred blessed,
To share the fond and kind embrace,
   Of those I once caressed.

If cheered with news of such a kind,
   I could here no longer stay,
But leaving copperheads behind,
   Go joyfully away.

If they again would peace restore,
   Invited back to come,
Though copperheads behind me roar,
   I soon should be at home.

THE PARTING SCENE.

How sad and solemn was the day,
I left my home and went away,
 It made my heart feel sore,
To leave my friends and kindred near,
A lovely wife and children dear,
 With all to meet no more.

The light of day away had passed,
The vail of night was o'er us cast,
 A bosom heaving band,
As each in kind and faithful aid,
A hasty preparation made,
 To take the parting hand.

Amid the scene of haste and care,
Arrived the time of holding prayer,
 Isaiah's tenth was read;
Though quite descriptive and sublime,
Much suited well the present time,
 As if to us 'twas said.

Swiftly the moment's passed away,
That brought the time to read and pray,
 And seek for aid divine;
Give thanks to God for mercies past,
And ask his guidance to the last,
 All to his care resign.

May he o'er heart and life preside,
With truth and graceforever guide,
 Till we are called to die;
And if on earth we meet no more,
May we beyond this gloomy shore,
 Meet round his throne on high.

The Holy Father's happy home,
Where grief and trouble never come,
 Forever there remain;
His glory view through endless days,
Sing highest anthems to his praise,
 And know that all is gain.

Oh, may we, if it be thy will,
All meet to dwell together still,
  The righteous race to run;
But if we cannot this obtain,
May all the loss to us be gain,—
  Thy righteous will be done.

Where'er we stay, where'er we roam,
In distant lands or near at home,
  Till we shall meet again.
The grace of him in whom we died,
To holy life and victory guide,
  Be thine the praise, Amen.

The evening prayer is ended now,
Oh, as we were no more to bow,
  Again to work we turn;
The stream of time glides swiftly by,
The parting scene is drawing nigh,
  And hearts will in us burn.

Attention now again is drawn,
It is to notice little John,
  For it was softly said,
As one to me did kindly tell:
"He wishes you to bid farewell,
  And then to go to bed."

He upward turned his little face,
As we enjoyed the last embrace,
  And took the parting kiss.
Oh, how it moved my inmost heart,
Thus with the tender child to part,
  At such a time as this.

Then on his head my hand I laid,
And silently to heaven prayed,
  That God the child would bless.
That he would store him well with grace,
To fill in life some useful place,
  Enrobed in righteousness.

I saw no more of little John,
For very soon the child was gone,
  And was composed in sleep;

While all the rest together stand,
And kindly press the parting hand,
   But none were heard to weep.

Though feeling deep possessed the heart,
And prospects sad increased the smart,
   Above all said before ;
The thing that yet would give us pain,
Was told in words both faint and plain,
   We all shall meet no more.

The parting scene I must regard,
While standing in the homestead yard,
   Beneath a spreading oak ;
Mid hearts with painful prospects rent,
And anxious thoughts that wanted vent,
   Though few the words we spoke.

The best advice I then could give,
Was all in Christ to try to live,
   Though union here must cease;
And we assunder still must stay,
Till some by death are called away,
   We yet shall meet in peace.

The things that most impressed my mind,
Upon my wife I then enjoined :
   To train the children right.
The words we last together spoke,
Were heard beneath the spreading oak,
   Near nine o'clock at night.

(The night before the oldest son,
From friend and native land had run,
   To keep his hands from blood,
And thus escape confederate laws,
That called to aid in treason's cause.
   And give insult to God.)

The state in which I then was placed,
Required care and watchful haste,
   To shun the rebel foe.
The moon had showed her solemn face,
And lunar day shined o'er the place,
   While I from home did go.

The parting scene I can't forget
Tis brilliant in my memory yet,
  For this my heart is sore:
Then last I saw a daughter's face,
Who now is held in death's embrace,
  On earth we meet no more.

Her careful eyes and thoughtful brow,
In vision rise before me now,
  As they did there appear;
Herself to me she cannot show,
But I to her must shortly go,
  With friends and kindred dear.

If in the Savior's happy home,
She is to rest till we shall come,
  Why should I sigh or mourn?
While here a stranger round I roam,
In distant lands away from home,
  From friends and kindred torn.

I still would wait upon the Lord,
Confiding in his holy word,
  May I no duty shun;
While I my calling will fulfill,
And suffer all his righteous will,
  Till I my race have run.

Nor from mine object turn my eyes,
Till I by grace have won the prize,
  Nor once at ease sit down,
Till every foe is conquered quite;
And I have fought the victor's fight,
  And well secured a crown.

THE WANDERING REFUGEE.

How oft my busy thoughts do fly,
To view the place where kindred lie.
  Who crossed cold Jordon's waves;

Where oft beneath the forest shade,
In youth I read and sang and prayed,
 But now a place of graves.

Just in that place or one near by,
The old and young together lie,
 The leader and the lead;
Who once in life had prospects fair,
In joy and sorrow both did share,
 But now are with the dead.

With whom I spent my youthful days,
And shared their night and morning lays,
 And joined in solemn prayer;
Those who had watched my infant sleep,
My youth in ways of truth did keep,
 And thus for good prepare.

And some for whow I did the same,
To train for him from whom they came,
 There together lie,
With branches of the ancient stock,
And members of my father's flock,
 And those to us less nigh.

Those ancient ones their race have run,
Though they their task on earth have done,
 Their labors are not gone,
For plainly where their offspring go,
They there their righteous training show,
 And thus their works go on.

And those who train as God decreed,
Shall all be honored by their seed,
 This truth they well shall know;
That those who children rightly train,
Shall see their labor was not vain,
 That they shall rightly go.

And though the fathers all are dead,
Their labors still shall go ahead,
 To make the saints complete;
When time her course has fully run,
With all their works on earth have done,
 They shall at judgment meet.

How sweet the rest of young and old,
Of whom I here have something told,
　If they in Jesus sleep,
Away from scenes of war and dread,
That through a sinful land have spread,
　Where thousands groan and weep.

The Lord my life doth still prolong,
And lead my heart to solemn song,
　As homeless here I stay;
Where'er the Lord my lot may cast,
Until his wrath be over, passed,
　And I am called away.

Now oft my heart is full of care,
And then goes forth in fervent prayer,
　To all my friends at home;
While on the Lord I still depend,
And wonder where the scene will end,
　And I shall cease to roam.

Departed friends still come to mind,
And cause me oft to feel inclined,
　As one of old did crave;
Where those the Lord hath greatly blessed,
Do now from pain and labor rest,
　That there may be my grave.

Where oft was found a calm retreat,
In winter mild and summer's heat,
　To be alone a while,
To read the sacred pages o'er,
The Lord for grace divine implore,
　And seek a Savior's smile.

In calm retreat and silent shade,
Were night and morning offerings made,
　Where none but God could hear;
His needful grace thus to derive,
Sad evils from the heart to drive,
　And make it all sincere.

Nor his good spirit thence withhold,
Nor leave to sin and Satan sold,
　Forsaken and alone.

But there his kingdom will maintain,
O'er all within forever reigns,
  And keep it for his own.

With holy light all through it shine,
To keep in sight the will divine.
  His image there impressed,
Till all the task of life is done,
And ends the race beneath the sun,
  Then take me home to rest,

With him who once was crucified,
And in the room of sinners died,
  Their just desert to bear;
To raise them from the depths of woe.
To them his wonderous grace to show.
  All things with him to heir.

A PROSPECTIVE SCENE.

THE FIRST PART WAS WRITTEN ABOUT THE BEGINNING OF THE WAR.

Lo! in a wide extended plain,
  Not ruled by righteous law,
Where most unhallowed passions reign,
  A mighty host I saw,

In wrath and spite and hellish strife,
  With mortal hate engage,
And woful scenes and loss of life,
  Fill the historic page.

While far around from side to side,
  From low and high degree,
Did freely flow the crimson tide,
  To form one common sea.

Where mangled heaps of low and high,
  Of every hue and class,

—17

Disolved in putrefaction lie,
    All moldering in a mass;

Where vapors foul pollute the air,
    Was once their dying groans,
Now holllow skulls that widely stare,
    And mangled, naked bones.

Whence strife and toil and life are fled,
    And all their mortal pains,
The wasting slumbers of the dead,
    A mournful sight remains.

Where once was mode the dying prayer,
    Mid doleful groanings round,
Which did most solemnly declare,
    That God on man had frowned.

Of such a scene as this beware,
    When in the field of blood,
An awful season to prepare.
    To meet an angry God.

Now do you ask the reason why
    Doth God with anger burn?
Unto his holy word apply,
    And there the reason learn.

SECOND PART.

His precepts there in order stand,
    As saints of old did oft rehearse,
And those who break his wise command,
    Incur his wrath and woful curse.

Those who by parents lightly set,
    And can their rightful claims despise,
Their blood must pay the awful debt,
    And birds of prey pick out their eyes.

Their blood the thirsty fowls refresh,
    That come from far the feast to share,
And hungry beasts consume their flesh,
    Once pampered much with pride and care.

The Lord in judgment on them roared,
　　Again their flesh to dust be sent,
Declining strength of earth restored,
　　Which they in pride and folly spent.

And thus the Lord in judgment reigns,
　　And brings the proud and lofty low,
The way of wicked men restrains,
　　And makes the unbelieving know.

The Lord among the nations rules,
　　And order from confusion brings,
Gives sober sense to crazy fools,
　　And humbles haughty, wicked kings.

To their right mind again restored,
　　When all ambitious hopes are lost,
To be at peace they can afford,
　　When wealth and life have paid the cost.

The terms they once could not admit,
　　As either wise, or just or good,
They tamely now to them submit,
　　When signed and sealed with human blood.

ERRATA.

EXPLANATION.—t stands for line from the top, and b from the bottom of the page.

On the 3d line tp 15, for excuses read exercises; on the 14th 1 tp 17, insert, after a subject of, and 8th b p read I for and. On the 6th line t p 20, for the read this. 2d l t p 23, for oh read ah, and 5th O. 15th l b p 23, for the read their. 1st l p 25, read him after sought. 22nd l t p 25, read so intolelable. 5th l t p 27, for policy read felicity; l 21st t p, for me read one. 6th l of prose t p 28, omit and after devilish ; in 8th l add d to practice; read pistol for Bible in last verse. 9th l t p 30, read one not ones; 11th b p 30, omit and. 14th l b p 34, omit and; and 3d b p, read without, 23d l p 35, for is read are. 4th l b p 37, for of read for, 18th l t p 41, lacks the quotation mark. 6th l t p 42, for hallow read hollow ; in last l p 42, for void read vain. 21st l b p 45, for one read persons ; 11th l b p 50 of prose, for pure read poor. Two lines at bp 50, lacks the quotation mark; 18th l t p 51, for Christ read church. 9th l b p 55, for may read any. 18th l p 62, for beefsteak read brutish. 3d l b p 63, for there read these. After rule in the 4th l b p 64, the great specific in, is left out. 1st l t p 65, for fork tongued read forked. 6th l t p 65, for exposed read expressed. On 2d and 3d l t p 71, read but for she, and let her, after to ; 19th l t p 71, for him by, read by him for. 3d l t p 73, omit that. 5th l p 74, read nearly. 19 t p 76, add called after were; and 18th l b p, for whose lives read which. In 2d verse of poem p 81, for wars transpire read war to inspire ; 1st line of 3d verse, for furthermore read for their own ; the first line of 6th verse should end with s ; the 4th should have a, not to. 2d l t p 82, for present read pleasure ; 7th of prose tp 82, add of the ocean, after bottom ; and in the 16th t p, read confederate before states. 8th l b p 83, for escape read cease. 15th l t p 85, for we read who. 20th b p 86, add in favor, before of. 6th l t p 88, for wanted to read would. 14th from b p 88, read and for I. 5th l t p 100, for morning read evening; and 12 b p, read was for is ; omit and in 18th. Read and for I, 17 l b p 101. 12th l t p 102, read I for and. 10th l b p 109, for Street read Stnt; and on 4th l b p read church. 14th l t p 110, omit sold. 3d l b p 111, for clean read doth clear. 2d l t p 112, read and for or. 19th l t p 120, add as, after and. 18th l b p 120, for l read and ; close with same and begin the next paragraph thus: Whether from curiosity or otherwise. 7th l t p 121, for get read set, and add him. 17th l t p, for a read I ; from 4th to 9th l's b p, should have been left out. 17th l b p 124, omit we. 15th l b p 128, read Bement; 12th l b p Bondurents; 6th l from b p read thus for I think. 6th l t p 129, for Etmire's read Etnire's where I. 13th l b p 131 Funderburg's· 19 l b p 134, read from Villa, &c. 1st l on p 140, begin with Z ; and in 9th tp, read woe ; begin last line of 4th verse with Gone. 5th l t p 143 read troubling; and 18th t p, read hill. 17lh t p 144, omit had. In 3d l of 1st verse p 148, omit and, insert a comma. 19th l t p 150, read of. 14th l b p 152, omit no. To 5th l t p 155, prose, add written. Last l 3d verse p 186, for flow read strow; 1st l 6th v same p for when I shall, read when shall I, &c.

www.ingramcontent.com/pod-product-compliance
Lightning Source LLC
Chambersburg PA
CBHW032134160426
43197CB00008B/643